effortless aga cooking

Food preparation:
Sarah Whitaker
Food styling:
Sarah, Clementine and Daisy Whitaker and Simon and Jenny Burgess
(all the photographs are of the actual recipes and once we had finished, we ate the lot!)
Photographs:
Simon Burgess

There is probably no such thing as an original recipe. If I have inadvertently duplicated anyone else's ideas, I apologise – sometimes I think there must be a spy in my kitchen when I see a television cook make a dish that I thought I had invented the day before!

Details of demonstrations, further copies of this book and copies of Sarah's other recipe collections:

Casual Aga Cooking

Relaxed Aga Cooking

and

The Twelve Days of Aga Christmas

are available from:

The Trout, Nether Wallop, Hampshire, SO20 8EW
e mail: kitchen@sarahwhitaker.com
www.sarahwhitaker.com
www.theagalady.com

effortless aga cooking

sarah whitaker
with photographs by
simon burgess

for Anthony, with love
and
for Daisy, Clementine and James, uncomplaining guinea pigs!

'Aga' and 'Rayburn' are registered trademarks of Aga Rangemaster plc

'Bake-O-Glide'™ is a reusable non-stick, coated cooking material manufactured by Falcon Products Ltd and available from cookshops and from Aga shops

A catalogue record for this book is available from the British Library.

ISBN 978-0-9554306-4-0

Published in Great Britain by Sarah Whitaker
The Trout, Nether Wallop, Stockbridge, Hampshire, SO20 8EW
www.sarahwhitaker.com

Photographs by Simon Burgess
www.simonburgessphotography.com

contents

getting to know your aga or range cooker

It is perfectly possible to cook on an Aga for 30 years and never use any of the cast iron cooking techniques. Lots of people do. They may wonder why the cooker loses heat, but love the cooker so much that they don't mind, much. Then they learn a few simple techniques, keep the lids down and cook more in the ovens and – as if by magic – the cooker stops losing heat and they never look back. If this is you, read on . . .

Life with an Aga is like a friendship. Its warm, benign presence in the kitchen is such a comfort in the house. It will cook any food you want, quickly or slowly, perfectly. From a slow-roasted Christmas turkey to a piece of toast, it is the ultimate cooker. For some people, it is the cast iron monster in the kitchen, frightening in the extreme – all those doors and no visible controls, where on earth do you start?

Put simply, an Aga has two hot plates: the left hand *boiling plate* is very hot – it boils. The right hand *simmering plate* is about half the temperature of the boiling plate – it simmers. The two-oven Aga has a top *roasting, oven* which is very hot – it roasts – and a lower, *simmering, oven* that is about half the temperature of the roasting oven – it simmers. The three-oven Aga has an additional *baking oven* that runs at a perfect temperature for baking, about half way between the roasting and simmering ovens. The four-oven Aga also has a *warming oven*, cooler than the simmering oven. And that's it.

The Aga is a heat storage cooker; it maintains heat until the lids are opened for too long or cool food is put into the ovens, when the thermostat kicks in and the heat gradually regenerates. Eighty per cent of all cooking on an Aga takes place in the ovens, saving heat and fuel. This has the added benefit of no spitting fat to clear up and no cooking smells – the ovens are vented to the flue and all smells just disappear up the chimney.

You should never need to turn it up or down – don't go near that dial, except to vacuum away the dog hairs occasionally! Please don't turn the Aga up if you are cooking for a party – you will only burn things, as it will be much hotter than you are used to! It may cook a little more slowly if the ovens are very full, but it will be consistent and reliable.

Many of these recipes refer to hanging the tins and shelves from the runners at the sides of the ovens. Always count the runners downwards from the top of the oven. Hanging roasting and baking tins from the runners uses less space – you can fit much more into the ovens at once!

a note about ingredients

I have deliberately not specified organic, free range or unrefined ingredients in my recipes. The choice is up to you, the cook.

I prefer to use good quality, seasonal, locally produced fresh ingredients, rather than those imported from around the world, out of season and context. I am not convinced that all imported 'organic' foods meet the strict UK standards. For example, I use local bacon in preference to imported pancetta, as I can see pigs in the fields nearby.

I will not use any ingredient that I cannot easily buy locally – it seems so unfair to say Baothat a recipe will only work if you use particular herbs gathered by fairies in the Provençal moonlight or a certain brand of olive oil only available from one Italian delicatessen in a back street in Islington or through the internet!

That said, I am very fortunate to live on the Hampshire/Wiltshire border, where wonderful farmers' markets, fresh fish and traditional butchers are found in abundance.

preparing ahead

In many of these recipes I have said that the food can be prepared ahead – to be cooked and either kept warm, or cooled and reheated to eat later or the next day.

Many of these dishes freeze really well, either part-cooked, or ready to defrost and serve. I tend to wrap dishes for freezing in kitchen paper, which absorbs any liquid given off during defrosting, to save things from becoming watery.

This does not mean that you *have* to make things in advance, just that you can, if it suits you to do so.

tomato tartlets

To feed more people: Re-roll the pastry and cut a further two or three rounds from the pack, allow a couple of extra tomatoes and you have 9 tartlets with a slightly thinner layer of cream cheese

Serves 6 as a starter, or serve two per person as a main course for 3

1 packet (375g) ready-rolled puff pastry
4 tomatoes
1 egg, beaten
7 oz (200g) pack cream cheese
1 tbsp fresh pesto

Oven:

Roasting oven, 200C, 400F, Gas 6

Prepare in advance:

Assemble the tartlets and chill for up to 24 hours before baking

Prepare ahead:

Keep the tartlets warm in the simmering or warming oven for up to half an hour

Freeze:

No, the tomatoes shrivel up as they are reheated

1. Set the pack of cream cheese onto the back of the Aga to soften.
2. Unroll the pack of pastry onto a work surface and cut out six 4"/25cm rounds with a cutter. Make a second circle inside the round with a cutter one size smaller, but do not press right through the pastry. This will make an edge to rise around the tomatoes.
3. Lay a sheet of Bake-O-Glide onto the cold plain shelf. Put the pastry rounds onto the Bake-O-Glide. Brush the edges of the pastry with beaten egg.
4. Mix together the cream cheese and pesto and spread onto the inside of the pastry rounds. Slice the tomatoes and lay the slices onto the cheese.
5. Set the plain shelf onto the floor of the roasting oven for about 10 minutes, until puffed up and golden with a crispy base.
6. Serve at once, with a scattering of chopped parsley or basil to show you have made an effort!

smoked salmon soufflés

To feed more people: Double the ingredients will fill 16 ramekins (if you have that many!)

Serves 8

4 oz (120g) pack smoked salmon trimmings
2 oz (55g) butter
1 oz (25g) plain flour
½ pint (300ml) milk
3 oz (85g) mascarpone
3 eggs
1 lemon
Salt and pepper
2 tbsp grated Parmesan cheese

Oven:

Roasting oven, 200C, 400F, Gas 6

Prepare in advance:

Cooked, cooled soufflés will keep in the fridge for up to 48 hours

Prepare ahead:

Either eat as soon as they are cooked, or cool and reheat for 10 minutes from the fridge

Freeze:

Yes, defrost and reheat for 15 minutes

1. Set the pack of mascarpone onto the back of the Aga to soften. Put the butter into a pan and set it on the back of the Aga to melt.
2. Brush 8 ramekins with the melted butter, then put some grated Parmesan into each and shake to cover the butter. Put the prepared ramekins into the small roasting tin.
3. Stir the flour into the remainder of the butter, then blend in the milk. Bring to the boil, stirring all the time until you have a thick white sauce. Season well and allow to cool a little.
4. Separate the eggs and whisk the whites until firm.
5. Beat the egg yolks into the white sauce, then stir in the softened mascarpone and the smoked salmon, plus any left over Parmesan.
6. Fold the beaten egg whites into this mixture, then pile it into the prepared ramekins.
7. Hang the tin from the 4th, lowest, runners in the roasting oven for about 15 minutes until they have puffed up and browned.
8. Serve at once, before they collapse.
9. OR, allow to cool and deflate, then chill or freeze until needed. Turn out of the ramekins and reheat in the roasting oven for 10 minutes until they puff up again. Serve the twice-baked soufflés with a dollop of sour cream and a sprig of dill.

chicken mousselines with tarragon sauce

To feed more people: Make smaller spoonfuls of mixture to stretch it round 7 or 8. Double the mixture will make enough mousselines for 16

Serves 6 as a starter, 4 for lunch!

1lb (450g) boneless, skinless chicken breasts
3 egg whites
½ pint (275ml) double cream
Salt and pepper

Sauce:

½ pint (275ml) chicken stock
¼ pint (150ml) cream
1 tbsp (5ml) brandy
1 tbsp (5g) chopped fresh tarragon
Salt and pepper

Oven:

Boiling plate, floor of roasting oven

Prepare in advance:

Uncooked chicken mixture will keep in fridge for 24 hours

Prepare ahead:

Will keep warm in simmering or warming oven for an hour

Freeze:

Yes

1. Put the chicken meat, egg whites, cream and seasoning into a processor and whizz to a pulp.
2. Bring a large pan of water to the boil and drop spoonfuls of the mixture into the water. Cover and simmer for about 7 minutes, until they float to the surface.
3. Lift the mousselines from the pan with a slotted spoon and dry on kitchen paper. Keep warm in the simmering oven until needed.
4. For the sauce: Tip all the ingredients into a pan and set on the floor of the roasting oven. Leave to boil and reduce by about half.
5. Serve the mousselines with the sauce poured over.

asparagus and pea mousse

The quintessential taste of an English summer

To feed more people: Rather than using double the ingredients, just make two to serve up to 20

Serves 8–10

1 bunch asparagus –
about 12oz (345g)
8 oz (220g) natural yogurt
12 oz (345g) peas (can be frozen)
Large handful mint leaves
3 egg whites
½ tsp sugar
Salt and pepper
Juice ½ lemon
4 tsp powdered gelatine
2 tbsp water

Tomato vinaigrette:

3 tbsp olive oil
1 tbsp lemon juice
2 tomatoes
Salt and pepper
½ tsp brown sugar
¼ tsp Dijon mustard

Oven:

Boiling plate

Prepare ahead:

Mousse will keep in the fridge for up to 24 hours

Freeze:

No, it collapses when you defrost it!

1. Trim the woody parts from the asparagus and cut into 1"/2½cm pieces. Bring a large pan of salted water to the boil and add the peas and asparagus. Cook for 2 minutes then drain and plunge the vegetables into a bowl of very cold water. Drain again and plunge into fresh cold water.
2. Mix the lemon juice and water in a jam jar and sprinkle on the gelatine. Leave to soak for a few minutes then stand in a pan of boiling water until dissolved.
3. Put the asparagus and peas into a food processor, with the yogurt, gelatine mixture and seasonings. Whizz in short bursts until well mixed but not puréed. Whisk the egg whites and fold in the asparagus and pea mush. Pour into an oiled 2lb/1kg loaf tin and chill until set.
4. For the tomato vinaigrette, pour boiling water over the tomatoes, leave for a minute then plunge into a bowl of cold water. Peel, quarter and remove pips. Chop into ¼"/5mm dice. Mix together other ingredients and add tomatoes.
5. Turn out the mousse and serve in slices, with a spoonful of tomato vinaigrette.

wondrous mushrooms

This works well as a canapé – the stuffing will fill up to 30 smaller mushrooms

Serves 6

6 large field mushrooms

Stuffing:

7 oz (200g pack) cream cheese

Juice ½ lemon

3 tbsp lumpfish caviar

½ tbsp fresh dill

Salt and pepper

1 tbsp chopped parsley

Cocktail sticks to serve

Oven:

Roasting oven, 200C, 400F, Gas 6

Prepare in advance:

24 hours, uncooked

Prepare ahead:

Will keep warm in simmering or warming oven for half an hour

Freeze:

No, the mushrooms go rubbery as they defrost

1. Set the pack of cream cheese onto the back of the Aga to soften.
2. Wipe the mushrooms and remove their stalks.
3. Line the small roasting tin with Bake-O-Glide and arrange the mushrooms in the tin with the open sides upwards.
4. Put the caviar into a sieve and hold under a running tap until the water runs clear, then drain.
5. Beat the cream cheese, lemon and dill together, add the caviar.
6. Pile the stuffing into the mushrooms and hang the tin from the 4th, lowest, runners in the roasting oven for about 15 minutes until the cheese mixture is puffed up and golden.
7. Serve at once, sprinkled with a little chopped parsley.

smoked salmon cake

To use this cake as a canapé, use only three pancakes and two layers of salmon in each cake tin and when chilled and set, cut into 1"/2cm squares

Serves 6

For the pancakes:

4 oz (110g) plain flour

1 egg

¼ pint (150ml) milk

Filling:

12 oz (375g) smoked salmon slices

2 tbsp dill sauce

1 pack (200g) cream cheese

Salt and pepper

1 lemon

1 tbsp parsley

Oven:

Simmering plate

Prepare in advance:

Will keep in the fridge for up to 24 hours

Freeze:

Yes

1. First, make the pancakes (or buy them!). Put the flour into a bowl and add the egg. Mix together, then slowly mix in the milk and beat until it is a smooth batter.
2. Either heat a greased frying pan and pour about 4 tbsp of the batter into the pan and swirl round, then cook until the top is no longer shiny, flip the pancake over and cook the other side, then turn onto a cooling rack and repeat until all the batter has been used up (you will get about 8 thin pancakes in an 8"/20cm pan), or put a piece of Bake-O-Glide onto the simmering plate and pour about 4 tbsp of the batter onto it, spread with a palette knife into a round pancake. Cook until the top is no longer shiny, flip the pancake over and cook the other side, then turn onto a cooling rack and repeat until all the batter has been used up.
3. Set the pack of cream cheese onto the back of the Aga to warm up and soften.
4. Mix together the cream cheese, seasoning and dill sauce.
5. Line an 8"/20cm cake tin with cling film. Put a pancake into the tin. Spread a spoonful of the cheese mixture over the pancake, then cover with smoked salmon and another pancake.
6. Repeat until you have five pancakes and four layers of smoked salmon. Cover with more cling film and chill for about an hour until set.
7. Turn the cake out onto a plate, decorate with wedges of lemon and a scattering of chopped parsley and serve in slices.

smoked cod roulade

To feed more people: Roll the roulade along its long side and slice into 12 narrow slices. To serve as a canapé, halve the roulade lengthways and roll into two long, thin roulades

Serves 8–10

5 oz (170g) smoked cod fillet
4 eggs
Salt and pepper

Filling:

Salt and pepper
1 tbsp sun dried tomato paste
7 oz (200g pack) cream cheese
2 tomatoes

Oven:

Baking oven,
180C, 350F, Gas 4

Prepare in advance:

Cooked, cooled and filled roulade will keep in the fridge for 24 hours

Freeze:

Yes, ready to serve but wrapped in kitchen paper to absorb moisture

1. Line the large roasting tin with Bake-O-Glide.
2. Separate eggs and whizz smoked cod, seasoning and yolks together to a paste.
3. Whisk the whites until firm and fold into the fish mixture. Spread this over the prepared tin.
4. 2 oven Aga: Hang the tin from the 4th runners in the roasting oven and the cold plain shelf on the 2nd runners. Bake for about 8 minutes.
5. 3 and 4 oven Aga: Hang the tin from the 3rd runners in the baking oven and bake for about 10 minutes.
6. When the roulade is cooked, turn out onto a tea towel, remove the Bake-O-Glide and roll up in the towel, to create a fat sausage. Allow to cool.
7. Scald the tomatoes in boiling water for 1 minute, then cool under the running cold tap. Peel off the skins, cut into quarters and scoop out the core and seeds. Chop into tiny (1/8"/3mm) dice. Beat the cream cheese with the sun dried tomato paste and stir in the diced tomatoes. Unroll the roulade and spread with the filling. Roll up tightly in the tea towel and chill for at least 4 hours.
8. To serve, cut into ½"/1cm slices and arrange on a plate.

scallops with cauliflower

To feed more people: Double the ingredients will feed up to 10 – allow three scallops per person

Serves 4

1 head cauliflower
3 tbsp crème fraîche
2 oz (55g) grated Cheddar cheese
Salt and pepper
12 scallops
1 clove garlic
1 tbsp olive oil
1 tbsp lemon juice
Chopped parsley to serve

Oven:

Simmering oven, 130C, 250F, Gas 1 and simmering plate

Prepare in advance:

Prepare the cauliflower and chill for up to 24 hours

Prepare ahead:

Cauliflower will keep warm in simmering or warming oven for an hour or so, marinate the scallops but cook them just before serving

Freeze:

No

1. Trim and prepare the cauliflower, put into a heavy pan and cover with water. Bring to the boil and when boiling hard, drain off all the water, cover and put into the simmering oven for 20 minutes to soften.
2. Take the cooked cauliflower from the oven and whizz to a purée, adding the crème fraîche, cheese and seasoning. Keep warm until later.
3. Crush the garlic into a bowl, add the oil, lemon juice and scallops. Leave for a few minutes to marinate.
4. Put a piece of Bake-O-Glide onto the simmering plate and put the scallops on. Turn after about 2 minutes, when they should be caramelised underneath.
5. Serve dollops of the cauliflower purée with the scallops and their garlic liquid on top. Finish with some chopped parsley to show you have made an effort!

chicken balls

Makes about 50, to serve as a starter for 6 or as canapés on cocktail sticks

1 lb (450g) chicken breast meat
4 oz (110g) bread
3 oz (85g) ground almonds
4 oz (110g) ready to eat dried apricots
2 eggs
2 tbsp fresh tarragon
2 tbsp soy sauce
Salt and pepper

Oven:

Roasting oven
200C, 400F, Gas 6

Prepare in advance:

Will keep in the fridge for up to 24 hours

Prepare ahead:

Will keep warm in simmering or warming oven for half an hour

Freeze:

Yes, uncooked

1. Pile all the ingredients into a food processor and whizz until well chopped and mixed.
2. With wet hands, roll into walnut sized balls and arrange on the large grill rack.
3. Line the large roasting tin with Bake-O-Glide.
4. Put the rack into the tin, pour water to cover the base and cover with foil.
5. Hang the tin from the 4th runners in the roasting oven and bake for 20–25 minutes and then pile into a serving dish.
6. Serve with tarragon dip.

tarragon dip

Makes about ½ pint (275ml)

3 tbsp mayonnaise
2 tbsp crème fraîche
1 tbsp chopped tarragon
1 tsp soy sauce
Salt and pepper

Prepare ahead:

Will keep in the fridge for up to 24 hours

Freeze:

No

Mix all ingredients together and serve.

cheese crisps

Makes about 20

4 oz (110g) mature Cheddar cheese
2 oz (55g) ready salted crisps
2 oz (55g) plain flour
2 oz (55g) butter

Oven:

Baking oven, 190C, 375F, Gas 5

Prepare in advance:

Will keep in a tin for up to 24 hours

Prepare ahead:

Will keep warm on top of the closed Aga lid for up to an hour

Freeze:

Uncooked only

1. Set the butter in a bowl on the back of the Aga to melt.
2. Line the cold plain shelf with Bake-O-Glide.
3. Grate the cheese and crush the crisps and tip into the bowl of melted butter. Add the flour and mix to form a dough.
4. Place heaped teaspoons of the mixture onto the plain shelf. Flatten with the back of a spoon.
5. 2 oven Aga: Slide the shelf onto the 4th runners in the roasting oven and bake for 10 minutes.
6. 3 and 4 oven Aga: Slide the shelf onto the 2nd runners in the baking oven and bake for 12–15 minutes.
7. Cool on a rack and serve.

hot cheese dip

Almost a fondue, but less stringy!

Serves 6

1 white cob loaf
½ pint (275ml) white wine
8 oz (230g) Gruyère cheese
1 oz (25g) plain flour
4 tbsp Kirsch liqueur
1 oz (25g) butter
Salt and pepper
1 tbsp chopped parsley
2 loaves French bread

Oven:

Simmering oven, 130C, 250F, Gas 1

Prepare in advance:

Not really, the cheese dip sets solid if refrigerated!

Prepare ahead:

Cheese dip will keep warm in simmering or warming oven for up to an hour

Freeze:

Bread only

1. Cut the top off the cob loaf and pull out all the crumb, leaving a hollow shell. Put into the simmering oven for half an hour to dry out.
2. Grate the cheese.
3. Melt the butter in a heavy pan on the simmering plate, then stir in the flour and blend in the wine. Bring to the boil, stirring all the time. Remove the pan from the heat.
4. Season, then add the cheese and kirsch and stir until melted – do not allow the mixture to boil once the cheese has been added.
5. Pour the cheesy goo into the hollowed out loaf, sprinkle with parsley and serve with thinly sliced French bread to dip into the cheese.

chilled watercress and apple soup

To feed more people: Double the ingredients will feed up to 9, or 12 in smaller bowls

Serves 4

1 medium onion

2 oz (55g) butter

1 bunch watercress

1 tbsp garam masala

1 pint (550ml) chicken stock

1 tbsp cornflour

¼ pint (150ml) double cream

2 egg yolks

2 dessert apples

Juice ½ lemon

Oven:

Simmering oven, 130C, 250F, Gas 1

Prepare ahead:

Cooked, cooled soup will keep in the fridge for up to 24 hours

Freeze:

No

1. Peel and chop the onion. Set the bowl of cream onto the back of the Aga to warm up.
2. Melt the butter in a heavy based pan and add the onion. When sizzling, cover and transfer to the simmering oven for 10 minutes to soften.
3. Move the pan of cooked onions to the simmering plate and stir in the garam masala and cook for a minute. Stir in watercress and stock. Mix cornflour with 2 tbsp/30ml water and add to the soup, then bring it to the boil. Cover again and transfer to the simmering oven for a further 10 minutes.
4. Peel, core and grate the apples, and pour over the lemon juice to prevent them from browning.
5. Remove the pan of soup from the oven and set on a work surface away from the Aga.
6. Mix the egg yolks with the cream, and add to the soup, taking care not to boil the mixture, as it will separate. Add one grated apple. Stir well. Season and chill.
7. Serve garnished with the remaining grated apple and a few watercress leaves.

leek and potato soup

To feed more people: Double the ingredients will fill up to 10 slightly smaller soup bowls

Serves 4–6

3 leeks
1 medium potato
1 oz (25g) butter
1 medium onion
2 cloves garlic
1 tbsp olive oil
1½ pints (800ml) stock

4 tbsp cream
Chopped parsley to garnish

Oven:

Aga simmering oven, 130C, 250F, Gas 1

Prepare in advance:

Will keep in the fridge for up to 48 hours

Prepare ahead:

Keep warm in the simmering oven for an hour

Freeze:

Yes, before adding cream

1. Peel and finely chop the onion and garlic. Slice the leeks. Cut the potato into small cubes.
2. Melt the butter and oil together in a heavy based pan and add the onion and garlic. Stir over the heat until sizzling. Cover and put into the simmering oven for 15 minutes to soften. Add the leeks and potato to the cooked onions. Stir in the stock, bring to the boil then cover and return to the simmering oven for 25 minutes.
3. Whizz in a food processor, then stir in the cream and pour into individual bowls.
4. Serve with a scattering of chopped parsley on top.

sweet potato and chestnut soup

This needs a really good stock, turkey is perfect!

To feed more people: Double the ingredients will make enough soup for 12, or 15 if served in small bowls

Serves 6

1lb (450g) sweet potatoes
2 large onions
2 cloves garlic
1 tbsp olive oil
2 pints (1¼ litres) strong stock
1 pack (200g) prepared chestnuts
Salt and pepper

To serve:

4 tbsp cream
1 tbsp chopped parsley

Oven:

Simmering oven, 130C, 250F, Gas 1

Prepare in advance:

Will keep in the fridge for 48 hours

Prepare ahead:

Keep warm in simmering or warming oven for an hour or so

Freeze:

Yes

1. Cut the sweet potatoes into chunks and peel and chop the onions and garlic.
2. Heat the oil in a heavy based pan on the boiling plate and add the vegetables and shake to coat them in the oil.
3. When the contents of the pan are sizzling, cover and transfer to the simmering oven for 10 minutes to soften.
4. Move the pan back to the boiling plate and add the stock and chestnuts. Season and bring to the boil, then cover again and transfer back to the simmering oven for about 30 minutes until all the vegetables are soft.
5. Purée the soup, then serve with a swirl of cream and a scattering of chopped parsley.

pea and watercress soup

To feed more people: Double the ingredients will fill up to 10 slightly smaller soup bowls

Serves 4

1 onion

1 clove garlic

1 tbsp olive oil

1 medium potato

1 pint (550ml) stock

8 oz (225g) frozen peas

4 oz (110g) bunch watercress

Sprig of fresh mint

¼ pint (150ml) double cream

Salt and pepper

Oven:

Simmering oven, 130C, 250F, Gas 1

Prepare in advance:

Cooked, cooled soup will keep in fridge for 24 hours

Prepare ahead:

Will keep warm for half an hour in the simmering or warming oven

Freeze:

Yes

1. Peel and chop the onion, crush the garlic and chop the potato into small chunks.
2. Heat the oil in a heavy pan on the simmering plate and add the onion, garlic and potato. Stir over the heat until sizzling, then cover and transfer to the simmering oven for 10 minutes to soften.
3. Move the pan to the boiling plate and add the stock, peas, mint and watercress. Bring to the boil and simmer for a minute or two, then remove from the heat.
4. Whizz the soup until smooth, add half of the cream and season before serving with a swirl of cream and mint leaf in each bowl.
5. Serve hot or cold.

Aga tip – use a couple of spoons of the liquid from slow-roasting a ham to make a pea, ham and watercress soup

roasted tomato and pepper soup

To feed more people: Double the ingredients will fill up to 10 slightly smaller soup bowls

Serves 4

1½lb (700g) ripe tomatoes
2 red peppers
2 red onions
2 cloves garlic
Handful fresh basil leaves
2 tbsp olive oil
1 large potato
2 pints (1 litre) stock
1 tbsp sun dried tomato paste
1 tbsp sherry vinegar
Salt and pepper

Oven temp:

Aga roasting oven, 400F, 200C,
Gas 6 and simmering oven

Prepare in advance:

Cooked, cooled soup will keep in the fridge for 24 hours.

Prepare ahead:

Will keep warm in simmering oven for an hour or so

Freeze:

Yes

1 Halve the tomatoes and peppers. Remove pith and pips from peppers. Peel the onions and cut into wedge shapes. Crush the garlic. Line the large roasting tin with Bake-O-Glide and tip in the vegetables, sprinkle over the oil and a few basil leaves. Hang the tin from the 2nd runners in the roasting oven and bake for about ½ hour.

2 Meanwhile, dice the potato and put into a large pan with the stock, tomato paste, sherry vinegar and seasoning. Bring to the boil. Cover and transfer to the simmering oven to soften.

3 When all the ingredients are tender, combine them and liquidise. Serve garnished with more basil leaves.

tomato and salami salad

To feed more people: Double the ingredients will make 8 portions, or more if served as part of a larger buffet

Serves 4

3 large beef tomatoes
4 spring onions
1 tbsp fresh basil leaves
1 tbsp balsamic vinegar
2 tbsp olive oil
4 oz (100g) salami in one piece
Salt and pepper

Oven:

Simmering plate

Prepare in advance:

Prepared tomatoes and onions will keep in the fridge, but the salami is nicest still warm

Prepare ahead:

Keep the salami warm for up to half an hour in the simmering or warming oven and the rest of the salad in the fridge, mix together just before serving

Freeze:

No

1. Cut the tomatoes into chunks and put into a bowl.
2. Wash and trim the spring onions, slice and add to the tomatoes.
3. Tear the basil leaves and add to the bowl.
4. Cut the salami into small cubes and tip into a frying pan. Set the pan onto the simmering plate and cook the salami until the fat runs and it begins to brown. Stir in the vinegar and oil, then tip into the tomatoes and mix well.
5. Serve at once.

Alternatives:

- Use spicy chorizo instead of the salami
- Use a finely chopped mild Spanish onion instead of the spring onions

spiced rice salad

To feed more people: Double all of the ingredients will serve up to 15 as part of a buffet, or 10 to accompany a cold meal

Serves 4–6

8 oz (225g) long grain rice (half a pint in a measuring jug)
1 large onion
1 clove garlic
1 tbsp olive oil
½ tsp ground turmeric
½ tsp ground cumin
Salt and pepper
¾ pint (450ml) chicken stock or water
4 oz (110g) dried apricots
2 oranges
3 tbsp French dressing
1 bunch spring onions
2 oz (50g) toasted flaked almonds
2 tbsp chopped parsley

Oven:

Simmering oven, 130C, 250F, Gas 1

Prepare ahead:

Cooked, cooled salad will keep in the fridge for up to 24 hours, but serve at room temperature

Freeze:

No

1. Grate the pith and squeeze the juice from the oranges. Chop the apricots and add to the orange juice and rind.
2. Peel and chop the onion. Crush the garlic. Heat the oil in a heavy based pan on the simmering plate and add the chopped onion and garlic. When sizzling, cover and transfer to the simmering oven for 10 minutes to soften.
3. When the onion is soft, add the rice and spices, stirring to coat thoroughly. Pour on the stock and bring to the boil. Cover and put back into the simmering oven for at least 15 minutes.
4. When the rice has absorbed all of the liquid, remove from the oven, stir in the French dressing and leave to cool completely.
5. Slice the spring onions finely and stir into the rice, with the apricots and oranges and flaked almonds. Sprinkle with chopped parsley and serve.

melon and cucumber salad

Serves 4

1 honeydew melon

1 lb (450g) tomatoes

1 large cucumber

1 handful each fresh mint and parsley

Salt and pepper

3 tbsp French dressing

Oven:

Boiling plate for the kettle!

Prepare ahead:

Prepare and mix the fruit together up to 3 hours in advance, but do not dress until just before serving

Freeze:

No

1. Cut the melon in half. Remove the seeds and scoop out the flesh with a melon baller, or cut into ¼"/5mm cubes.
2. Boil a kettle and pour boiling water over the bowl of tomatoes. Leave for a minute, then drain and cool under a cold running tap for another minute. Skin, quarter and remove the seeds from tomatoes.
3. Peel the cucumber and cut into cubes, the same size as the melon.
4. Mix all the fruit together, pour the dressing over and sprinkle with chopped mint and parsley.

Aga tip: Keep your kettle empty. Fill with as much fresh cold water as needed for that cup of coffee or bowl of tomatoes, then discard any left in the kettle afterwards - an empty kettle cannot scale up!

scallop, prawn and bacon salad

To feed more people: Serves up to 6 on small plates! Double the ingredients will feed 8, or up to 12 on small plates

Serves 4

8 – 12 scallops, depending on whether this is a main course or a starter!
8 oz (225g) raw peeled prawns
4 rashers smoked bacon
1 onion
1 clove garlic
1 lemon
Bag (150g) mixed salad leaves
2 tbsp olive oil
2 tbsp lemon juice
Salt and pepper

Oven:

Simmering plate

Prepare in advance:

Cook the onions and bacon, which will keep in the fridge for up to 24 hours, but cook the scallops and prawns just before serving

Prepare ahead:

Not really, the shellfish need to be eaten as quickly as possible after cooking

Freeze:

No

1. Peel and chop the onion, crush the garlic and cut the bacon into chunks.
2. Pile the salad leaves onto a pretty serving plate.
3. Heat 1 tbsp of the oil in a heavy based pan and add the onion, garlic and bacon. Set the pan onto the simmering plate and stir over the heat for about 5 minutes – the bacon will sizzle and crisp up, the onions will begin to brown.
4. Put the scallops and prawns into the pan and stir over the heat for a minute or two until the prawns change colour from grey to pink.
5. Add the rest of the oil and the lemon juice, stir and then tip the hot mixture onto the salad. Grate over the rind of the lemon. Serve immediately, right now, as the leaves will wilt quickly.
6. *If this is for a main course, serve with new potatoes or crusty bread.*
7. *If you cannot eat this as soon as it is cooked, use a mixture of Chinese leaves and iceberg lettuce, which do not collapse as quickly as other leaves.*

bean and barley salad

To feed more people: Serves up to 8 if part of a large buffet

Serves 4

8 oz (225g) mixed pulses and pearl barley – usually sold as 'soup mix' in a bag together
1 tbsp vegetable stock powder
Bunch spring onions
1 red chilli
1 clove garlic
2 tbsp chopped fresh parsley
2 tbsp chopped fresh coriander

Dressing:

3 tbsp olive oil
1 tbsp balsamic vinegar
Salt and pepper

Oven:

Simmering oven, 130C, 250F, Gas 1

Prepare in advance:

Will keep in the fridge for 24 hours

Freeze:

No, the dressing and herbs go slimy

1. Put the bean and barley mix into a bowl and cover with cold water. Leave to soak for 12 hours or overnight.
2. Drain the beans and tip into a pan. Cover with cold water and add the stock powder. Bring to the boil, then cover and move to the simmering oven for 30 minutes.
3. Take the cooked beans from the oven, drain them and leave to cool.
4. Trim and chop the onions, crush the garlic and chop the chilli.
5. Mix the dressing (shaken in a jam jar is easiest) and pour over the cold beans, then stir in the spring onions, garlic, chilli and herbs.
6. Serve at room temperature.
7. *Do not add the herbs to the salad until it is completely cold, as the dressing reacts with the herbs and they will go brown.*

asparagus and parma ham salad

To feed more people: Double all of the ingredients will serve up to 9, especially if served on small plates!

Serves 4

8 oz (225g) fresh asparagus

4 oz (110g) sliced Parma ham

1 oz (25g) fresh Parmesan cheese

6 oz (175g) mixed salad leaves

1 tbsp olive oil

Dressing:

2 tbsp olive oil

1 tbsp balsamic vinegar

½ tsp sugar

Salt and pepper

Oven:

Roasting oven, 200C, 400F, Gas 6

Prepare ahead:

Wrapped asparagus will keep in the fridge for 24 hours uncooked

Freeze:

No

1. Line a small shallow baking tray with Bake-O-Glide.
2. Trim the asparagus and slice the ham into long strips.
3. Mix together the dressing ingredients (in a jam jar is easiest).
4. Lay the strips of ham onto a work surface and roll a spear of asparagus in each strip – sounds fiddly but it is very quick!
5. Put the wrapped asparagus into the tin and hang from the top set of runners in the roasting oven for about 5 minutes, until the ham is crispy and the asparagus tender.
6. Toss the salad leaves in the dressing and divide between four plates. Put the cooked asparagus onto the leaves and grate over the fresh Parmesan.
7. Serve at once.

halloumi and orange salad

To feed more people: Double the ingredients will serve up to 10

Serves 4

2 packs (250g each) Halloumi cheese
3 oranges
2 oz (55g) pecan nuts
1 bag (150g) mixed rocket salad
Handful mint leaves
3 tbsp olive oil
1 tbsp white wine vinegar

Oven:

Simmering plate

Prepare in advance:

Prepare the oranges and chill for up to 24 hours

Prepare ahead:

Best eaten as soon as it is ready

Freeze:

No

1. Cut the halloumi into even slices.
2. Using a very sharp knife, cut the top and bottom off each orange, then pare off the rind and pith. Cut out the segments from the oranges and put into a bowl – do this over the bowl, to catch the juice as it drips when you cut the segments. Add the vinegar and oil to the bowl and mix well.
3. Tip the salad into the bowl of dressing, add the nuts and tear in the mint leaves. Toss everything together then arrange on individual plates.
4. Put a piece of Bake-O-Glide onto the simmering plate and lay the slices of halloumi onto it. Cook for 2–3 minutes on each side, until the cheese is golden brown.
5. Put the cheese onto the salad and pour over the dressing. Serve at once.

spiced cauliflower and potato

To feed more people: Double the ingredients will feed up to 9, or more if part of a curry buffet

Serves 4

- 1 medium onion
- 1 clove garlic
- 1 tbsp olive oil
- ½ tsp turmeric
- 1 tsp ground cumin
- 1 tsp garam masala
- ½ tsp salt
- 1 tin (230g) chopped tomatoes
- 3 potatoes
- 1 medium cauliflower
- 1 tbsp dry white vermouth

Oven:

Simmering oven, 130C, 250F, Gas 1

Prepare in advance:

Cooked, cooled casserole will keep in fridge for 24 hours

Prepare ahead:

Will keep warm for a further hour or so in the simmering or warming oven

Freeze:

Yes

1. Peel and chop the onion, crush the garlic. Cut the potatoes into even sized chunks and divide the cauliflower into small florets.
2. Heat the oil in a heavy pan on the simmering plate, add the onion and garlic and once it is sizzling, cover and transfer to the simmering oven for about 10 minutes to soften.
3. Transfer the pan to the simmering plate and stir in the spices and salt. Stir over the heat for a minute, then add the tomatoes, potatoes, cauliflower and vermouth.
4. Cover the pan and move to the boiling plate until it is bubbling, then transfer to the simmering oven for about three quarters of an hour until the vegetables are tender.
5. Serve scattered with chopped parsley, to show you have made an effort!

Aga tip: Make sure the lid is on properly – if the steam can escape, the contents of the pan will not cook in the simmering oven

fennel and tomato crumble

To feed more people: Double the ingredients will fill a large sauté pan and will feed up to 10, especially if served with barbecued sausages

Serves 4

2 tbsp olive oil
4 fennel bulbs
2 cloves garlic
1 medium onion
½ pint (300ml) tomato passata
½ tsp balsamic vinegar

Crumble:

3 slices bread
1 oz (25g) grated Parmesan
2 oz (55g) grated Cheddar cheese
The trimmings from the top of the fennel bulbs
3 oz (85g) pecan nuts

Oven:

Roasting oven, 200C, 400F, Gas 6

Prepare in advance:

Assemble the crumble and chill for up to 24 hours in the fridge before baking

Prepare ahead:

Will keep warm for up to an hour in the simmering or warming oven

Freeze:

Yes

1. Peel and chop the onion and garlic. Trim the fronds from the top of the fennel bulbs (keep these for the crumble) and then slice the bulbs.
2. Heat the oil in a 9"/24cm sauté pan or casserole. Add the onion, garlic and fennel and cover with a lid. When the lid is hot to touch, the contents of the pan are cooking, so transfer the pan to the simmering oven for about 30 minutes to soften.
3. When the vegetables are soft, move the pan to the boiling plate and remove the lid. Pour in the passata and vinegar, season well and stir well. Remove from the heat.
4. For the crumble, tip all the ingredients into a processor and whizz to crumbs. Pour this over the top of the vegetables.
5. Hang the grid shelf on the second runners in the roasting oven and put the pan onto it.
6. Bake for about 15 minutes until the top is golden brown and crisp.
7. Serve with tomato salad and crusty bread.

pancakes

Don't just keep pancakes for Shrove Tuesday, they are a quick and easy starter all year round

Makes about 8

4 oz (110g) plain flour

1 egg

½ pint (275ml) milk

1. Beat together the flour, egg and milk until it is a fine batter. Allow to stand for a few minutes.
2. Put a large circle of Bake-o-Glide onto the simmering plate. Pour about 2 tbsp of the batter onto the simmering plate and spread out to the edges. When the surface is bubbling, flip over using a fish slice to cook the other side.
3. Serve at once, with a squeeze of lemon juice and a sprinkling of sugar, or fill to make a more substantial dish!

pancake fillings:

roasted vegetables

1 red pepper

1 courgette

½ aubergine

1 medium onion

2 cloves garlic

1 tbsp olive oil

2 oz Cheddar cheese, grated

Oven:

Roasting oven, 400F, 200C, Gas 6

Prepare ahead:

24 hours

Freeze:

Yes

1. Wash and trim the vegetables, then cut into even sized pieces. Toss in the oil and season well, then tip into a roasting tin and hang from the second set of runners for about 30 minutes until browned and softened.
2. Fill the pancakes with the roasted vegetables and roll up each one. Set into an oven proof dish, scatter over the cheese and bake for a few minutes until the cheese is bubbling and golden.

sautéed garlic mushrooms pancake filling

You could serve this on toast, without the pancakes! Try it on top of a griddled steak or stirred into cooked chicken breasts

Serves 4

4 oz (110g) button mushrooms
1 tbsp olive oil
½ oz (15g) butter
3½ oz (100g) pack Boursin garlic and herb cheese

Oven:
Floor of roasting oven

Prepare ahead:
24 hours

Freeze:
Yes

1. Set the cheese onto the back of the Aga to warm and soften.
2. Wipe and quarter the mushrooms. Melt the butter and oil in a heavy based frying pan on the simmering plate (cast iron or removable handle aluminium) and add the mushrooms. Heat until sizzling, then transfer to the floor of the roasting oven for 5–10 minutes until the mushrooms are cooked. Put the pan back on the simmering plate, tip in the cheese and stir until melted.
3. Fill the pancakes with the creamy mushrooms and roll up each one. Serve with a little chopped parsley scattered over.

mushroom risotto

To feed more people: Double the ingredients will feed 8

Serves 4

½ pint (300ml) in a measuring jug risotto rice
2 tbsp olive oil
1 onion
2 cloves garlic
1 pack (50g) dried mushrooms
2 tbsp dry white vermouth
8 oz fresh mushrooms
1 oz (25g) butter
Salt and pepper
2 oz (55g) fresh Parmesan

Oven:

Simmering oven, 130C, 250F, Gas 1

Prepare in advance:

Will keep in the fridge for up to 24 hours

Prepare ahead:

Will keep warm in simmering oven for an hour or two

Freeze:

Don't see why not!

1. Put the dried mushrooms into a jug and pour over a pint (550ml) of boiling water. Leave to stand.
2. Peel and chop the onion and crush the garlic.
3. Heat the oil in a heavy based pan and add the onion and garlic. When sizzling, cover and transfer to the simmering oven for 10 minutes to soften.
4. Move the pan of cooked onions to the simmering plate. Stir in the rice and vermouth, and add the dried mushrooms and their stock. Bring to the boil, then cover and return to the simmering oven for about 20 minutes until the rice has absorbed all the liquid.
5. Slice the fresh mushrooms and put into a pan with the butter and set it on the simmering plate. Toss the mushroom slices in the butter until they are cooked, then stir them into the risotto.
6. Grate the Parmesan over the risotto and serve.

Aga tip: Measure the rice – a beer mug is a pint and will feed 8, a coffee mug is half a pint and will feed 4, a ramekin is ¼ pint and will feed two and an egg cup is enough for one. Use the same vessel to measure the liquid – two measures of liquid to one of rice for risotto

potato and onion cake

To feed more people: Double the ingredients in a 11"/28cm sauté pan will serve up to 10. Half the ingredients in an 8"/20cm frying pan will feed 2–3

Serves 4

4 oz (110g) butter

2 large onions

1½ lb (650g) Maris Piper potatoes

1 tsp vegetable stock powder

1 tbsp mixed dried herbs

Salt and pepper

Oven:

Roasting oven, 200C, 400F, Gas 6

Prepare in advance:

Assemble and cook the dish and keep in the fridge for up to 24 hours in advance

Prepare ahead:

Will keep warm (but the base will not be especially crisp) in the simmering or warming oven for up to an hour

Freeze:

Yes

1. Peel and slice the onions. Set half of the butter in a large bowl on the back of the Aga to melt.
2. Heat the rest of the butter in a 9"/24cm sauté pan on the boiling plate and add the onions. When sizzling, cover and transfer to the simmering oven for 10 minutes to soften.
3. While the onions are in the oven, slice the potatoes as thinly as possible – in a processor or with a mandolin or with a sharp knife! Put the sliced potatoes into the bowl with the melted butter and add the stock powder and herbs and season well.
4. Tip the cooked onions into the bowl of potatoes and mix well.
5. Put the mixture into the sauté pan and press down firmly. Put on the lid.
6. Set the pan onto the floor of the roasting oven for 10 minutes to brown the base, then move onto the grid shelf on the 3rd runners and bake for a further 20 minutes until the potatoes are soft.
7. To serve, turn out the potato cake onto a plate and cut into wedges.

courgette bake

To feed more people: Double the ingredients in a 11"/28cm sauté pan will serve up to 10. Half the ingredients in an 8" frying pan will feed 2–3

Serves 4

3 medium courgettes
1 large onion
1 carrot
3 oz (85g) Cheddar cheese
4 oz (110g) self raising flour
3 fl oz (85ml) vegetable oil
5 eggs
Salt and pepper

Oven:

Baking oven, 160C, 350F, Gas 4

Prepare ahead:

Will keep warm in the simmering or warming oven for half an hour

Freeze:

No

1. Peel and chop the onion.
2. Grate the cheese, carrot and courgettes.
3. Break the eggs into a large bowl, and beat in the flour, oil and seasoning. Add the chopped onion, grated carrot, courgettes and cheese and mix thoroughly.
4. Pour into an ovenproof dish and bake.
5. 2 oven Aga: Set the dish into the large roasting tin and hang it on the 4th runners in the roasting oven. Slide the plain shelf onto the 2nd runners above and bake for about 30 minutes until risen and golden.
6. 3 and 4 oven Aga: Slide the grid shelf onto the 4th runners in the baking oven and set the dish into it. Bake for about 30 minutes until risen and golden.
7. Serve with crusty bread and a green salad.

tomato and cheese muffins

Makes 12 large, 24 smaller or 36 mini muffins

8 oz (225g) self raising wholemeal flour
1 tsp baking powder
½ tsp bicarbonate of soda
½ tsp salt
2 oz (55g) Gruyère cheese
2 oz (55g) Aga-dried tomatoes (or semi dried tomatoes from a packet!)
1 pack (20g) basil leaves
¼ pint (150ml) milk
6 tbsp (75ml) olive oil
2 eggs

Oven:
Roasting oven, 190C, 375F, Gas 5

Prepare in advance:
Grate the cheese and chop the tomatoes, weigh everything out but mix and bake just before serving

Prepare ahead:
Hide the cooked muffins in a tin for 24 hours

Freeze:
Yes

1. Grate the cheese and cut the tomatoes into small pieces. Chop the basil.
2. Line a muffin tin with paper cases.
3. Tip all the ingredients into a large bowl and mix together.
4. Pour the mixture into the muffin cases and bake.
5. Set the grid shelf onto the floor of the roasting oven and put the muffin tin onto it. Bake for about 20 minutes until risen and browned. (Mini muffins will be cooked in about 15 minutes.)
6. Eat as soon as they are cool enough to handle!

daisy's quinoa bake

Serves 4

8 oz (225g) quinoa (measures ½ pint in a jug)
¾ pint (450ml) vegetable stock
1 tbsp olive oil
1 onion
1 clove garlic
8 oz (225g) broccoli
3 oz (85g) grated Cheddar cheese
3 oz (85g) mascarpone
Salt and pepper

Oven:

Simmering oven, 130C, 250F, Gas 1

Prepare in advance:

Will keep in the fridge for up to 24 hours

Prepare ahead:

Will keep warm in the simmering or warming oven for an hour

Freeze:

Yes

1. Measure the quinoa and stock, tip into a pan and bring to the boil. Cover the pan and transfer to the simmering oven for 15 minutes until all the liquid has been absorbed.
2. Peel and chop the onion, crush the garlic and divide the broccoli into bite sized florets.
3. Set the mascarpone onto the back of the Aga to soften.
4. Heat the oil and add the broccoli, onion and garlic. Stir over the heat until sizzling, then cover and transfer to the simmering oven for 10 minutes to soften.
5. Tip the softened broccoli and onion mixture into the pan of quinoa, stir in the softened mascarpone and season well. Turn this into an oven proof dish, scatter the cheddar over and put the dish as high as possible in the roasting oven for 10 minutes until the cheese has melted and browned.
6. Serve hot or warm.

three vegetable terrine

To feed more people: Make two terrines to feed 16, or cut into thinner slices to make 10 portions from each terrine

Serves 8

12oz (345g) sweet potato
2 tbsp double cream
2 cloves garlic
8 oz (225g) mushrooms
8 oz (225g) fresh spinach
Nutmeg
6 oz (175g) Cheddar cheese
6 eggs
Salt and pepper

Oven:

Roasting oven,
180C 375F, Gas 4

Prepare in advance:

Keep in the fridge for up to 24 hours, reheat to serve

Prepare ahead:

Will keep warm in simmering or warming oven for up to an hour

Freeze:

Yes, when cooked, defrost slowly as it will give off extra water as it defrosts

1. Grate the cheese and divide into 3 piles. Chop the sweet potato into 1"/2.5cm cubes. Put it into a pan of cold water with a peeled clove of garlic, bring to the boil then drain, cover and transfer to the simmering oven for about 20 minutes.
2. When the sweet potatoes are soft, whizz them with 2 eggs and a third of the cheese in a processor. Season and allow to cool.
3. Whizz the mushrooms with the remaining clove of garlic in a processor, then tip into a sauté pan and add the cream. Set the pan onto the floor of the roasting oven for about 10 minutes, until most of the liquid has boiled away. Whizz again, with a further third of the cheese and 2 eggs. Season and allow to cool.
4. Wash the spinach and drain thoroughly. Put into a pan and cook on the simmering plate until wilted – a minute or two – then drain, pressing out as much water as possible – a potato masher is useful here! Whizz with the last two eggs, final third of the cheese, a few grates of nutmeg and seasoning.
5. Line a 2lb (1kg) loaf tin with an opened out roasting bag. Pour the spinach purée into this. Smooth the top, then gently pour on the sweet potato mixture. Again, smooth the top before pouring on the mushrooms. Cover with oiled foil.
6. Put the loaf tin into a roasting tin and pour boiling water around the base, to a depth of an inch (2.5cm).
7. Hang the tin from the 4th runners in the roasting oven and bake for 40 minutes. Remove from the oven, allow to stand for 5 minutes, then turn out. Serve warm, in slices.

potato and tomato bake

To feed more people: Double the ingredients will feed 9

Serves 4

1½ lb (700g) waxy new potatoes
1 onion
2 cloves garlic
2 tbsp olive oil
3 tomatoes
Handful fresh basil leaves
½ pint (300ml) crème fraîche
4 oz (110g) Gruyère or Emmental cheese
Salt and pepper

Oven:

Simmering oven, 130C, 250F, Gas 1 and roasting oven, 200C, 400F, Gas 6

Prepare in advance:

Assembled dish will keep in fridge for 24 hours before baking

Prepare ahead:

Will keep warm for an hour in the simmering oven

Freeze:

Don't see why not!

1. Cut the potatoes into even sized chunks, about ½"/1cm across.
2. Put the potatoes into a pan and cover with cold water. Bring to the boil on the boiling plate and when they are boiling hard, drain off all the water, cover with a lid and put the pan into the simmering oven for about 30 minutes until the potatoes are soft.
3. While the potatoes are in the oven, peel and chop the onion and crush the garlic. Cut the tomatoes into chunks the same size as the potatoes.
4. Heat the oil in a pan and add the onion and garlic. When sizzling, cover with a lid and transfer to the simmering oven for about 15 minutes until softened.
5. When the onions are cooked, remove from the oven and add the tomatoes and the basil. Season well, then shake the pan over the heat for a minute or two, then add the cream and mix well.
6. Tip the cooked potatoes into an ovenproof dish and pour the tomato sauce over. Grate the cheese and scatter it over the top of the sauce.
7. Set the grid shelf on the 2nd runners in the roasting oven and put the dish onto it. Bake for about 20 minutes until the cheese is melted and browned and the sauce bubbling.
8. Serve with a few basil leaves torn over the top.

mushroom tart

To feed more people: Double the ingredients will fill a 12"/30cm flan dish and will cut into 12 portions

Serves 4–6

For the pastry:

6 oz (175g) plain flour
3 oz (85g) butter
1 tbsp Parmesan cheese
2–3 tbsp water

For the filling:

2 large onions
2 cloves garlic
8 oz (225g) mushrooms
1 tbsp olive oil
Salt and pepper
3 eggs
Small tub (200g) crème fraîche
3 oz (85g) Gruyère cheese

Oven:

Roasting oven, 200C, 400F, Gas 6

Prepare in advance:

Cooked, cooled tart will keep in the fridge for up to 24 hours

Prepare ahead:

Will keep warm in the simmering or warming oven for an hour

Freeze:

Yes, either just the raw pastry in its dish (fill and cook from frozen) or the finished, cooked, tart

1. To make the pastry, put the flour, butter and Parmesan into a processor and whizz until the texture of breadcrumbs. With the motor running, add the water a spoonful (10ml) at a time until it comes together as a dough.
2. Roll out the pastry and line a 9"/23cm flan dish. Chill or freeze until required.
3. For the filling, Peel and chop the onions and crush the garlic. Halve the mushrooms. Put into a heavy based pan with the olive oil and heat on the boiling plate until sizzling. Cover and transfer to the simmering oven for about 20 minutes to soften.
4. Beat the eggs and crème fraîche together and season well. Grate the cheese.
5. Pour the mushroom mixture into the prepared flan case. Pour the egg and crème fraîche mixture over. Scatter the cheese on the top.
6. Put the tart onto the floor of the roasting oven for about 25 minutes until the pastry is golden.

Aga tip: Heat the oil, onions, garlic and mushrooms in a covered pan and when the lid is too hot to rest your hand on, move it to the simmering oven without opening the lid – the contents of the pan will be at boiling point. No steam or cooking smells will escape into the kitchen

spinach and tomato tart

To feed more people: Double the ingredients will fill a 12"/30cm flan dish and will cut into 12 portions

Serves 4–6

For the pastry:

6 oz (175g) plain flour
3 oz (85g) butter
1 tbsp Parmesan cheese
¼ tsp grated nutmeg
2–3 tbsp water

For the filling:

8 oz (225g) fresh spinach
¼ tsp grated nutmeg
Salt and pepper
3 eggs
7 oz (200g tub) cream cheese
3 oz (85g) Gruyère cheese
4 oz (110g) cherry tomatoes

Oven:

Aga roasting oven, 200C, 400F, Gas 6

Prepare in advance:

Cooked, cooled tart will keep in the fridge for up to 24 hours

Prepare ahead:

Will keep warm in the simmering or warming oven for up to an hour, or cool slowly beside the Aga for an hour or so

Freeze:

Yes

1 Set the cream cheese onto the back of the Aga to soften.
2 To make the pastry, put the flour, butter, nutmeg and Parmesan into a processor and whizz until the texture of breadcrumbs. With the motor running, add the water a spoonful (10ml) at a time until it comes together as a dough.
3 Roll out the pastry and line a 9"/23cm flan dish. Chill or freeze until required.
4 For the filling, whizz the spinach to a paste in a processor. Add the cream cheese, Gruyère, eggs and seasonings and whizz again. Pour this green mixture into the prepared pastry case.
5 Scatter the cherry tomatoes and over the top of the spinach.
6 Put the tart onto the floor of the roasting oven for about 25 minutes until the pastry is golden.

Aga tip: No need to bake pastry blind in an Aga, the intense heat of the floor of the oven gives a brown crisp crust every time

mozzarella risotto

To feed more people: Double the ingredients will feed up to 8, or 10 as a starter

Serves 4

8 oz (225g) risotto rice
1 medium onion
1 clove garlic
1 tbsp olive oil
1 pint (550ml) vegetable stock
8 oz (225g) Mozzarella
3 oz (85g) Parmesan
2 oz (55g) butter
Few fresh basil leaves
1 tbsp chopped fresh parsley
Salt and pepper

Oven:

Simmering oven, 130C, 250F, Gas 1

Prepare in advance:

Cooked, cooled risotto will keep in the fridge for 24 hours

Prepare ahead:

Will keep warm in the simmering or warming oven for an hour or so

Freeze:

Yes

1. Peel and chop the onion and crush the garlic.
2. Heat the oil in a heavy pan on the simmering plate and add the onion and garlic. When the vegetables are sizzling, cover and transfer to the simmering oven for 10 minutes to soften.
3. Transfer the pan to the boiling plate, stir in the rice and stock and bring to the boil. Re-cover and return the pan to the simmering oven for at least 25 minutes.
4. Grate the cheeses together. The Mozzarella has quite a mild flavour and will need plenty of seasoning unless the stock is strongly flavoured.
5. When the rice has absorbed the stock, stir in the cheeses and herbs.
6. Serve as soon as possible, with a tomato salad.

Aga tip: Do not add the herbs until just before serving, as they will lose their vibrant green colour if kept in the simmering or warming oven for a long time

butter bean, olive and tomato bake

To feed more people: Double the ingredients will feed up to 9

Serves 4

2 x 400g cans butter beans
1 tbsp olive oil
2 red onions
8 oz (225g) piece chorizo sausage
2 cloves garlic
1 tsp turmeric
1 tsp ground cinnamon
1 tsp smoked paprika
8 oz (225g) cherry tomatoes
1 tsp sugar
3 oz (100g pack) pitted black olives
Chopped parsley to serve

Oven:

Simmering oven, 130C, 250F, Gas 1 and floor of roasting oven

Prepare in advance:

Cooked, cooled bake will keep in the fridge for 24 hours

Prepare ahead:

Will keep warm in simmering or warming oven for an hour or so

Freeze:

Don't see why not!

1 Open and drain the cans of beans.
2 Peel and slice the onions, crush the garlic and halve the tomatoes. Cut the chorizo into ½"/1cm cubes.
3 Heat the oil in a heavy pan and add the onions, chorizo and garlic. Stir over the heat until sizzling, then cover and transfer to the simmering oven for 10 minutes to soften.
4 Transfer the pan to the simmering plate and stir in the spices. Stir over the heat for a minute, then add the beans, olives and tomatoes.
5 Move the pan, uncovered, to the floor of the roasting oven for about 5 minutes until the tomatoes are tender.
6 Serve with a scattering of chopped parsley and some crusty bread.

For a vegetarian version, leave out the chorizo and add a can of haricot beans to stretch the dish

courgette burgers

Serves 4 as a starter or 2 as a main course

2 medium courgettes
2 tbsp self-raising flour
1 oz Grana Padano or other hard Italian cheese
Pinch smoked paprika
Salt and pepper
1 tbsp olive oil
Red pepper sauce (from a jar if you prefer) to serve!

Oven:

Floor of roasting oven

Prepare in advance:

Make the burgers and chill for up to 24 hours

Prepare ahead:

Will keep warm in simmering or warming oven for half an hour

Freeze:

No, the burgers get very watery as they defrost

1. Wash the courgettes, dry them, then grate them and the cheese into a bowl.
2. Stir in the flour and season well with salt, pepper and smoked paprika.
3. Heat the oil in a heavy pan on the boiling plate.
4. Take spoonfuls of the mixture and dollop into the pan.
5. Transfer the pan to the floor of the roasting oven and fry for about 4 minutes, then flip the burgers over and fry for a further 3 or 4 minutes.
6. Serve with red pepper sauce.

red pepper sauce

2 red peppers
1 orange
Tabasco sauce (optional)
Salt and pepper

Oven:

Roasting oven

Prepare in advance:

Will keep in the fridge for 24 hours

Prepare ahead:

Will keep warm for an hour in the simmering or warming oven

Freeze:

Yes

1. Put the peppers into a roasting tin and roast for 25 minutes, until blackened. Cover the tin and leave to cool.
2. Remove the skin from the peppers, cut open and remove the seeds.
3. Squeeze the juice from the oranges and whizz, with the peppers and a few drops of Tabasco and seasoning to taste.

leek and blue cheese risotto

To feed more people: Double the ingredients will feed 8, or 12 as a starter

Serves 4

8 oz (225g) risotto rice
1 lb (450g) leeks
1 clove garlic
2 tbsp olive oil
2 tbsp dry white vermouth
1 pint (550ml) vegetable stock
3 oz (75g) soft blue cheese – eg Roquefort, Gorgonzola
2 oz (55g) butter
1 tbsp chopped fresh parsley

Oven:

Simmering oven, 130C, 250F, Gas 1

Prepare in advance:

Cooked, cooled risotto will keep in the fridge for 24 hours

Prepare ahead:

Will keep warm in the simmering or warming oven for an hour or so

Freeze:

Yes

1. Wash and trim the leeks, then slice into rounds about the thickness of a pound coin. Crush the garlic.
2. Heat the oil in a heavy pan on the simmering plate and add the leeks and garlic. When the vegetables are sizzling, cover and transfer to the simmering oven for 10 minutes to soften.
3. Transfer the pan to the boiling plate, stir in the rice, vermouth and stock and bring to the boil. Re-cover and return the pan to the simmering oven for at least 25 minutes or up to 2 hours.
4. Crumble the cheese – you cannot grate blue cheese!
5. When the rice has absorbed the stock, stir in the butter, cheese and parsley.
6. Serve as soon as possible, with a tomato salad.

Aga tip: This has to be the most effortless way to make a risotto ever, no standing at the Aga stirring and stirring, it can practically be made from another room!

stilton cheesecake

To feed more people: Double the ingredients will fill a 10"/25cm tin and will cut into 10 slices, but it will need an extra 10 minutes in the oven

Serves 4

- 2 oz (55g) butter
- 8 digestive biscuits
- 6 oz (175g) Stilton
- 7 oz (200g pack) cream cheese
- 1 egg
- ½ tsp chopped fresh rosemary

Oven:

Baking oven, 180C, 350F, Gas 4

Prepare in advance:

Cooked, cooled cheesecake will keep in the fridge for 24 hours

Prepare ahead:

Leave cooked cake to cool slowly beside the Aga for an hour before serving

Freeze:

Yes

1. Set the butter onto the back of the Aga to soften or melt.
2. In a processor, whizz the biscuits to crumbs. Stir in the butter and whizz again.
3. Line a 7"/18cm tin with Bake-O-Glide. Press the biscuit mixture onto the base of the tin.
4. Put the Stilton, cream cheese, egg and rosemary into the processor (no need to wash the bowl) and whizz. Pour this mixture onto the biscuit base.
5. Bake the cheesecake for about 20 minutes until set.
6. 2 oven Aga: Set the tin into the large roasting tin and hang it from the 4th runners in the roasting oven. Slide the plain shelf onto the 2nd runners above.
7. 3 and 4 oven Aga: Set the grid shelf onto the floor of the oven and put the cake tin onto it.
8. Remove from the oven and leave to cool – it will firm up as it does so. Serve tepid or at room temperature.

gnocchi

Serves 6

2 lb (900g) floury potatoes

2 eggs

7 oz (200g) plain flour

Salt and pepper

Fresh nutmeg

Oven:

Simmering oven, 130C, 250F, Gas 1

Prepare in advance:

Prepared gnocchi will keep in the fridge for 24 hours before cooking

Prepare ahead:

Will keep warm in simmering or warming oven for up to an hour, longer with sauce on top

Freeze:

Yes

1. Cut the potatoes into even sized pieces and put into a large saucepan. Bring to a serious boil, then drain, cover and put into the simmering oven for at least half an hour to soften.
2. When the potatoes are soft, remove the lid and shake them about in the pan on the simmering plate for a few minutes to drive off any moisture.
3. Mash the potatoes thoroughly, then add the eggs, flour, seasoning and a few grates of nutmeg. Mix well, then turn out onto a board and knead to a smooth dough.
4. Divide the dough into lumps of about 4"/10cm, then roll each one into a long thin sausage shape, about an inch/2.5cm across.
5. Cut the sausages into 1 inch /2.5cm pieces. Flatten each piece with a fork to give the classic gnocchi shape.
6. Bring a large pan of water to the boil and drop in about a third of the gnocchi. After a while, they will float to the surface. Once all have floated, cook for a further minute then lift them out of the pan onto a plate lined with kitchen paper or a tea towel to drain, and put them into the warmed dish while you cook the second third of the gnocchi, and then repeat for the final batch.
7. Pour over some tomato sauce (or Bolognese or grated cheese and olive oil or whatever you fancy) and serve.

spinach gnocchi

Serves 6

1½lb (700g) spinach
12 oz (375g) Ricotta cheese
1 lemon
4 oz (110g) butter
2 eggs
3 tbsp plain flour
3 oz (100g) Parmesan cheese
Salt and pepper

Oven:

Simmering oven, 130C, 250F, Gas 1

Prepare in advance:

Prepared gnocchi will keep in the fridge for 24 hours before cooking

Prepare ahead:

Will keep warm in simmering or warming oven for up to an hour, longer with sauce on top

Freeze:

Yes

1. Grate the Parmesan.
2. Wash the spinach and put it into a large pan and cover. Set on the simmering plate and in about 3 minutes it will have wilted to almost nothing! Drain in a colander and press firmly (a potato masher is good for this).
3. When the spinach has been pressed to remove as much water as you can, return to the pan and shake about in the pan on the simmering plate for a few moments to drive off any more moisture. Chop the spinach.
4. Add the ricotta and about half of the butter to the pan of chopped spinach, grate in the lemon rind and stir over the heat for a few minutes, beating until it is soft. This takes seconds in a processor!
5. Remove from the heat and beat in the eggs and the flour and a couple of tablespoons of the grated Parmesan.
6. Line a small roasting tin with Bake-O-Glide and spread the mixture over it. When cool, chill for about an hour until firm.
7. Put a large serving dish into the simmering oven to warm up.
8. Divide the dough into lumps of about 4"/10cm, then roll each one into a long thin sausage shape, about 1 inch/2.5cm across. Cut the sausages into 1 inch/2.5cm pieces. Flatten each piece with a fork to give the classic gnocchi shape.
9. Bring a large pan of water to the boil and drop in about a third of the gnocchi. After a while, they will float to the surface. Once all have floated, cook for a further minute then lift them out of the pan onto a plate lined with kitchen paper or a tea towel to drain, and put them into the warmed dish while you cook the second third of the gnocchi, and then repeat for the final batch.
10. Pour over some tomato sauce (or Bolognese or grated cheese and olive oil or whatever you fancy) and serve.

green risotto

To feed more people: Double all of the ingredients will serve up to 8

Serves 4

12 oz (350g) broad beans
3 tbsp fresh, chopped herbs – parsley, marjoram, basil, tarragon, etc
1 oz (25g) butter
1 medium onion
1 clove garlic
1 tbsp olive oil
8 oz (225g) risotto rice
1 pint (550 ml) stock
1 lemon
3 oz (85g) freshly grated Parmesan

Oven:

Simmering oven, 130C, 250F, Gas 1

Prepare ahead:

Will keep warm in simmering or warming oven for up to an hour, don't add the herbs until just before serving as they will lose their colour as they wait

Freeze:

Yes

1. Blanche the broad beans in boiling salted water for 3 minutes, until just tender. Drain and refresh in cold water. If you wish, pop the beans out of their outer skins and use the inner bean only. Set aside.
2. If using frozen broad beans, just leave them beside the Aga to defrost while the rice cooks!
3. Roughly chop the onion and crush the garlic. Melt the butter and oil together in a sauté pan and add the onion and garlic. Cook on the simmering plate until sizzling, then cover and transfer to the simmering oven for 10 minutes to soften.
4. When the onion is soft, add the rice and the stock. Bring to the boil then cover and return to the simmering oven for about 25 minutes. The risotto should look creamy and the rice cooked.
5. Stir in the beans, herbs, Parmesan and grated rind and juice of the lemon. Serve at once.

leek pie

Serves 4–6

2 x packs (each 375g) ready-rolled puff pastry
2 oz (55g) butter
1 lb (450g) leeks
1 tub (200g) cream cheese
1 oz (25g) grated Parmesan
1 tbsp grainy mustard
1 egg

Oven:

Roasting oven, 200C, 400F, Gas 6

Prepare in advance:

Assemble the pie and chill for up to 24 hours before cooking

Prepare ahead:

Will keep warm in simmering or warming oven for half an hour, or serve tepid

Freeze:

Uncooked, assembled pie

1. Wash and trim the leeks, then slice into rounds about ¼"–½ cm across.
2. Set the tub of cream cheese on the back of the Aga to warm up and soften.
3. Melt the butter in a heavy pan in the simmering plate and add the leeks. Stir over the heat until the leeks are sizzling, then cover and transfer to the simmering oven for about 20 minutes until soft.
4. Take the cooked leeks from the oven and stir in the cream cheese, Parmesan and mustard. Leave to cool.
5. Line the plain shelf with Bake-O-Glide. Unroll one of the packs of pastry onto the shelf.
6. Brush the edge of the pastry with beaten egg.
7. Spread the cool leek mixture over the pastry, leaving an edge of about an inch.
8. Unroll the second piece of pastry and lay it over the top, pressing down around the edges to seal.
9. Brush the top of the pie with beaten egg, then put it onto the floor of the roasting oven for about 20 minutes until puffed up and golden.

Aga tip: Slide the Bake-O-Glide off the shelf straight onto the floor of the oven in one quick move. When the pie is cooked, lift the edge of the Bake-O-Glide and slide the shelf underneath to take the pie out of the oven

surprise green pasta

To feed more people: Double the ingredients will feed up to 9 – you may prefer not to double the chilli unless you want a bigger surprise!

Serves 4

- 9 oz (250g) penne pasta
- 9 oz (250g) fresh spinach
- 7 oz (200g tub) cream cheese
- 2 cloves garlic
- 1 green chilli
- ¼ tsp grated nutmeg
- Salt and pepper
- 3 tbsp grated fresh Parmesan to serve

Oven:

Boiling plate

Prepare in advance:

Sauce will keep in the fridge for up to 2 days

Prepare ahead:

Will keep warm in simmering or warming oven for half an hour

Freeze:

Sauce only

1. Peel and crush the garlic, trim the chilli.
2. To make the sauce: Put about two thirds of the spinach into a processor, with the cream cheese, garlic, chilli, nutmeg and seasoning and whizz to a lovely green sludge. Season well.
3. Cook the pasta in boiling water on the boiling plate according to the instructions on the packet.
4. Drain the cooked pasta and return it to the warm pan. Tip in the sauce and the remaining spinach, stir over the heat for a minute of two and serve with a scattering of fresh Parmesan on top.

squash pots

To feed more people: Pour less custard into each of 8 ramekins to feed 8, or double the ingredients will stretch around 16 small ramekins

Serves 6

1 butternut squash
1 tbsp olive oil
1 tub (300ml) crème fraîche
1 oz (25g) fresh grated Parmesan
2 eggs
Salt and pepper
Fresh nutmeg
1 tbsp fresh chopped parsley to serve

Oven:

Roasting oven, 200C, 400F, Gas 6, then baking oven, 160C, 350F, Gas 4

Prepare in advance:

Roasted squash will keep in the fridge for 24 hours. Cooked, cooled custards will keep in the fridge for 24 hours

Prepare ahead:

Set cooked custards beside the Aga for a couple of hours to cool down after cooking

Freeze:

No, the custard separates as it defrosts

1. Put the squash into the small roasting tin and hang from the 3rd runners in the roasting oven. Roast for about 45 minutes until tender. Remove from the oven and allow to cool.
2. Brush 6 ramekin dishes with the oil and put into the roasting tin.
3. Halve the cooked squash and remove the pips. Scoop the flesh from the skin – you will need about ½ pint (300ml, or a coffee mug full). Save the rest for soup or something!
4. Tip the squash into a processor, with the crème fraîche, cheese, eggs and seasonings – use a few grates of nutmeg. Whizz to a purée.
5. Pour the orange gloop into the ramekins and cover the tin with foil.
6. 3 and 4 oven Aga: Hang the tin from the 3rd runners in the baking oven.
7. 2 oven Aga: Set the tin in the large roasting tin and hang from the 4th runners in the roasting oven, and slide the plain shelf onto the 2nd runners above.
8. Cook for about 20 minutes until the custards are set but still a bit wobbly in the centre – they will firm up as they cool down.
9. Serve tepid or at room temperature, with a scattering of chopped parsley on top and a slice of crusty bread.

yorkshire pudding

Makes 12 individual puddings or 8 man-size ones!

2 eggs
4 oz (110g) plain flour
½ pint (300ml) milk
Pinch of salt
3 tbsp sunflower oil or dripping

Oven:
Roasting oven, 220C, 450F, Gas 7

Prepare in advance:
Cooked, cooled puddings will keep in the fridge for 24 hours

Prepare ahead:
Remove cooked puddings from the oven, leave to cool and then reheat for 5 minutes before serving

Freeze:
Yes, reheat from frozen in the roasting oven for about 10 minutes

1. Put the plain shelf into the roasting oven on the 3rd runners.
2. Put a little oil into each hole of a large muffin tin and set it on top of the plain shelf in the oven.
3. Put the eggs, salt and flour into a wide jug and mix to a paste. Add the milk a little at a time, whisking until it is all incorporated.
4. Pour the batter into the hot tin and bake on top of the heated shelf for about 15 minutes.
5. Cook your puddings before you roast your joint, when the oven is at its hottest, then leave them to cool and reheat just before serving.

Ring the changes:

- You could add some grainy mustard, chopped rosemary or other herbs to the batter.
- You could use beer instead of the milk in the batter
- Use half milk and half water in the batter if milk is short

Aga tip: Putting the plain shelf into the roasting oven before cooking the puddings raises the temperature above the shelf, trapping the hot air at the top of the oven

crunchy spiced potatoes

Serves 4

1½ lb (800g) King Edward potatoes
1 tbsp olive oil
1 onion
1 clove garlic
½ tsp smoked paprika
½ tsp ground cumin
½ tsp cayenne pepper
½ tsp salt
Small tub (100g) low fat crème fraîche
1 tbsp chopped chives

Oven:

Simmering oven, 130C, 250F, Gas 1 and floor of roasting oven

Prepare in advance:

Cooked potatoes will keep in the fridge for 24 hours, reheat in roasting oven

Prepare ahead:

Will keep warm for an hour in the simmering oven, transfer to boiling plate for a minute or two to crisp up before serving

Freeze:

Yes, reheat straight from the freezer

1. Cut the potatoes into 1"/2cm chunks. Peel and chop the onion, crush the garlic.
2. Put the potatoes into a pan and cover with cold water. Bring to the boil on the boiling plate, then drain, cover and transfer to the simmering oven for 10 minutes.
3. Heat the oil in a large sauté pan on the simmering plate, add the onion and garlic and stir over the heat. Cover and transfer to the simmering oven for 10 minutes to soften.
4. Transfer the pan of onions to the simmering plate and add the spices. Stir over the heat, then tip in the cooked potatoes.
5. Set the pan onto the floor of the roasting oven for 10 minutes, then shake it to turn the potatoes and return to the oven for a further 10 minutes.
6. Serve with cold crème fraîche and a scattering of chopped chives on top.

scented aga rice

Serves 4

½ pint (300ml) long grain rice
¾ pint (450ml) water
1 tsp black onion seeds
1 tsp cumin seeds
5 cardamom pods
½ tsp ground turmeric

Oven:

Simmering oven, 130C, 250F, Gas 1

Prepare ahead:

Will keep warm in simmering or warming oven for an hour or so

Freeze:

Yes, cool the cooked rice quickly

1. Measure the rice and water.
2. Tip rice, water and spices into a pan and bring to the boil.
3. Cover and transfer to the simmering oven for at least 12 minutes, or up to an hour or so.
4. When the rice is cooked, fluff it up with a fork and serve.

creamy mashed potatoes

Serves 4

1½ lb (600g) potatoes
¼ pint (150ml) creamy milk
1 oz (25g) butter
Salt and pepper
Grated nutmeg

Oven:

Simmering oven, 130C, 250F, Gas 1

Prepare in advance:

Will keep in fridge for up to 24 hours, reheat with a little more milk to soften

Prepare ahead:

Will keep warm in simmering oven for up to an hour

Freeze:

Yes

1. Cut the potatoes into even sized pieces. Put into a pan and cover with water. Bring to the boil on the boiling plate, drain, cover and put into the simmering oven for 35–45 minutes until soft. Drain again.
2. Mash, then add the milk, butter, salt, pepper and a good grating of nutmeg.
3. Beat until smooth and serve.

roasted spiced carrots

Serves 4–5

1lb (450g) carrots
2 tbsp sunflower oil
1 tbsp smoked paprika

Oven:

Roasting oven, 200C, 400F, Gas 6

Prepare ahead:

Allow to cool then reheat in roasting oven for about 5 minutes

Freeze:

Yes, reheat for about 8 minutes in roasting oven.

1. Line the small shallow baking tray with Bake-O-Glide.
2. Cut the carrots in half lengthways and remove the tops.
3. Pile into the roasting tin with the oil and smoked paprika. Shake well to coat with the oil.
4. Hang the tin from the second set of runners and roast for about 15 minutes, season and serve.

smoked haddock with horseradish cream

To feed more people: Allow one chunk of fish per person, double the rest of the ingredients will cover up to 10 pieces of fish

Serves 4

4 chunks of smoked haddock fillet
2 tbsp horseradish cream
3 tbsp crème fraîche
2 slices bread

Oven:

Roasting oven, 200C, 400F, Gas 6

Prepare in advance:

Prepared, uncooked fish will keep in the fridge for up to 24 hours

Prepare ahead:

Will keep warm in simmering or warming oven for about half an hour

Freeze:

Prepared, uncooked fish

1. Mix together the horseradish and crème fraîche. Whizz the bread into crumbs.
2. Line the small shallow baking tray with Bake-O-Glide.
3. Put the fish pieces into the tray, then spread the creamy horseradish over them.
4. Sprinkle the breadcrumbs over the coated fish, then bake.
5. Hang the tin from the second runners in the roasting oven for about 7 minutes until bubbling and crunchy.
6. Serve with new potatoes and a tomato salad or green vegetables.

sole mousseline

This may appear fiddly at first glance, but it is very quick and makes a lovely starter or could be served warm, with hollandaise sauce. If you chill it, the juices will set as a fishy jelly, so remember to take it out of the fridge an hour or so before eating

Serves 4 as a main course, 6 as a starter

2 filleted lemon soles, skinned

5 oz (150g) cooked prawns

½ pint (300ml) mayonnaise

Filling:

1 lb (450g) haddock, skinned

4 egg whites

½ pint (285ml tub) low fat crème fraîche

Salt and pepper

Watercress and slices of lemon to garnish

Oven:

Baking oven, 375F, 180C, Gas 4

Prepare in advance:

Cooked, cooled dish will keep in the fridge for up to 24 hours

Prepare ahead:

Will cool down slowly to room temperature for about 2 hours

Freeze:

Yes

1. Line a 2lb/1kg loaf tin with an opened out roasting bag. Lay the fillets in the mould, so that they overlap and overhang the edges. Chill until needed.
2. Put the haddock into a processor with the egg whites and crème fraîche. Season and whiz. Pour into the mould of sole, then fold over the edges of the fillets to envelop the filling. Cover with foil.
3. Set the loaf tin into the large roasting tin and pour in boiling water to about an inch (3cm) deep.
4. 2 oven Aga: Hang from the lowest set of runners in the roasting oven.
5. 3 and 4 oven Aga: Hang the tin from the second set of runners in the baking oven.
6. Cook for about 35 minutes until the filling is set. Remove from the oven and allow to cool.
7. Turn out onto a serving dish – you will need to mop up some of the juices with kitchen paper as they tend to overflow the plate if you are not careful!
8. Pile the prawns into the centre of the ring, garnish with watercress and slices of lemon and serve the mayonnaise separately. I like this served at room temperature, or even tepid!

smoked mackerel and spring onion tart

To feed more people: Double the ingredients will fill a 12"/30cm flan dish and will cut into 12 slices

Serves 4–6

6 oz (175g) plain flour
3 oz (85g) butter
1 tbsp Parmesan
2–3 tbsp water

4 oz (110g) smoked mackerel
3 tbsp horseradish sauce
4 spring onions
3 eggs
5 fl oz (150ml) milk
4 oz (110g) Cheddar
Salt and pepper

Oven:

Roasting oven, 200C, 400F, Gas 6

Prepare ahead:

Cooked, cooled tart will keep in the fridge for up to 24 hours

Prepare ahead:

Keep warm in simmering or warming oven for up to an hour

Freeze:

Yes, either the raw pastry in its dish ready to be filled and baked, or the complete cooked tart

1. To make the pastry, put the flour, butter and Parmesan into a processor and whizz until the texture of breadcrumbs. With the motor running, add the water a spoonful at a time until it comes together as a dough.
2. Roll out the pastry and line a 9"/23cm flan dish. Chill or freeze until required.
3. For the filling, roughly chop the mackerel and put it into the pastry case. Trim and slice the spring onions and scatter over the fish. Grate the Cheddar cheese into a bowl. Add the eggs and milk with the horseradish and a little salt and pepper and beat together.
4. Pour into the prepared flan case and put onto the floor of the roasting oven for about 25 minutes until set and golden.

smoked cod layer bake

To feed more people: Double all the ingredients will feed 8 people. Double the other ingredients, but triple the fish, will feed 12 people, but will need at least an hour in the simmering oven

Serves 4

½ oz (15g) butter
1 onion
4 oz (110g) bacon pieces
8 oz (225g) tomatoes
12 oz (375g) smoked cod fillet
2 tbsp dry white wine
Black pepper
1 or 2 slices bread
2 oz (55g) grated Cheddar cheese

Oven:

Roasting oven, 200C, 400F, Gas 6

Prepare in advance:

Cooked, cooled bake will keep in fridge for 24 hours

Prepare ahead:

Will keep warm in simmering oven for an extra hour

Freeze:

Yes, assembled and uncooked bake. Defrost and cook for an extra 5 minutes

1. Peel and slice the onions, slice the tomatoes. Cut the fish into four equal-sized pieces.
2. Heat the butter in a heavy based pan. Dip a piece of kitchen paper into the butter and use this to grease an ovenproof dish.
3. Add the bacon pieces and onions to the pan and when sizzling, transfer the pan to the floor of the roasting oven to brown for 5 minutes.
4. Put half of the sliced tomatoes into the dish. Tip the cooked onions and bacon on top of the tomatoes, then lay on the pieces of fish. Cover the fish with the remaining tomato slices. Pour over the wine and grate over a little pepper (no need for salt with the smoked fish and bacon!).
5. Crumble the bread over the top of the tomatoes, scatter the cheese on top and bake.
6. Slide the grid shelf onto the floor of the oven and set the dish onto it and bake for about 25 minutes until the top is golden brown.

sesame crusted tuna with sally's green sauce

To feed more people: Allow one chunk of fish per person. Double the sauce ingredients will stretch around 10

Serves 4

4 tuna steaks, about 4 oz (100g) each
2 tbsp sesame oil
4 tbsp sesame seeds
1 tbsp sunflower oil

Sauce:

2 cloves garlic
1"/2cm piece fresh ginger
4 spring onions
1 green chilli
3 tbsp light soy sauce
1 tbsp Thai fish sauce (nam pla)
Grated rind and juice of a lime
Handful fresh coriander

Oven temp:

Aga boiling plate

Prepare in advance:

Coated, uncooked fish will keep in the fridge for 24 hours, as will the sauce.

Prepare ahead:

Eat as soon as it is cooked

Freeze:

Yes, uncooked coated fish only

1. Tip the sesame oil into a wide, shallow bowl and the sesame seeds into another bowl.
2. Unwrap the tuna steaks and dry thoroughly on kitchen paper. Dip the steaks into the sesame oil, then into the seeds, so that the seeds stick to the steaks.
3. If time allows, put the coated steaks in the fridge to chill before cooking.
4. To make the sauce: Put all the ingredients into a processor and whizz together to make a bright green sauce.
5. Heat a heavy based pan on the boiling plate for a minute or two, then add the sesame oil and sunflower oil. Put in the tuna steaks and fry for a couple of minutes on each side, turning once.
6. Serve the crunchy steaks with noodles and a puddle of green sauce.

Aga tip: Sesame oil has a very low smoke point and will burn in the pan on the boiling plate, so always use it mixed with a more robust oil to prevent the smoke alarms going off in the kitchen

tuna with courgettes

To feed more people: Allow one tuna steak and up to one courgette per person, double the quantity of sauce will serve up to 12

Serves 6

6 tuna steaks
3 tbsp olive oil
4 medium courgettes
1 clove garlic
Salt and pepper

Sauce:

2 tbsp lemon juice
6 tbsp olive oil
2 tbsp chopped parsley
1 tbsp chopped oregano
2 tbsp capers, roughly chopped

Oven:

Floor of roasting oven

Prepare ahead:

No, this is best eaten as soon as it is cooked

Freeze:

No

1. Wash the courgettes and grate them, with the garlic. Heat a heavy pan in the roasting oven for 5 minutes, then pour in 3 tbsp oil and tip in the grated courgette and garlic, stir and then return to the floor of the roasting oven for 2–3 minutes. Stir once and continue to cook for a further minute or two. Tip into a serving dish and keep warm in the simmering oven.
2. Fry the tuna steaks in the same pan, on the floor of the roasting oven, for about 2–3 minutes each side until browned on the outside and still slightly undercooked on the inside.
3. For the sauce: Mix all the ingredients together (easiest in a jam jar).
4. Pile the courgettes onto plates, then lay a tuna steak on top of each pile. Spoon over the sauce and serve.

two fish terrine

This is a long recipe, but very spectacular for a dinner party starter

To feed more people: Make two terrines to serve 16, or cut thinner slices to serve 10 or 11 from one terrine

Serves 8

12 oz (345g) skinned cod or haddock fillet
2 tbsp water
1¼ lb (600g) skinned salmon fillet
4 oz (110g) thin green beans, trimmed
1 tub (200g) crème fraîche or low fat fromage frais
3 tsp powdered gelatine
1 tbsp lemon juice
Salt and pepper
½ pint (275ml) mayonnaise
2 tbsp chopped fresh dill

Oven:

Roasting oven, 400F, 200C, Gas 6

Prepare ahead:

Cook the fish up to 24 hours in advance, or prepare the terrine up to 24 hours in advance

Freeze:

Yes, terrine but not sauce

1. Put 2 tbsp of water and the lemon juice into a bowl and scatter the powdered gelatine over it. Set this onto the back of the Aga to melt.
2. Wrap the fish in separate foil parcels. Set these parcels into the large roasting tin and hang it from the 3rd runners in the roasting oven. Bake the cod for 10 minutes and the salmon for 20 minutes.
3. Remove the fish from the oven and allow to cool, then remove from the foil.
4. Bring a pan of water to the boil and tip in the beans. Boil for a minute, then drain and refresh in cold water. Drain and pat dry on kitchen paper.
5. Line a 2lb/1kg loaf tin with cling film.
6. Whizz the salmon with two thirds of the crème fraîche or fromage frais and two thirds of the gelatine and lemon mixture. Add seasoning. Pour half of this gloop into the prepared tin and chill until set.
7. Lay half the beans on the set salmon mixture. Whizz the cod with remaining crème fraîche or fromage frais and gelatine. Season. Pour onto the beans, then chill until set.
8. Lay the rest of the beans on the set cod mixture. Pour over the remaining salmon, smooth the top, cover with cling film and chill for at least 4 hours until really set.
9. Serve cut into slices, with a spoonful of mayonnaise, flavoured with the dill.

baked cod with sorrel crust

To feed more people: Allow one piece of fish per person and double the rest of the ingredients will cover up to 14 pieces of fish

Serves 6

6 skinless cod loin steaks
4 slices day-old bread
3oz (75g) butter
1 onion
1 clove garlic
Bunch of sorrel (or 85g bag of rocket)
Salt and pepper

Oven

Roasting oven, 200C, 400F, Gas 6

Prepare ahead:

Uncooked fish with crust on will keep in the fridge for up to 12 hours

Freeze:

Yes, uncooked fish with crust on

1. Wash and dry the fish steaks.
2. Peel and chop the onion, crush the garlic.
3. Melt the butter in a heavy based pan on the simmering plate and add the onion and garlic. When sizzling cover the pan and transfer to the simmering oven for 10 minutes until softened.
4. Tip the cooked onion and garlic into a processor and add the sorrel or rocket, bread and seasoning. Whizz until chopped and mixed.
5. Line a shallow baking tray with Bake-O-Glide.
6. Lay the cod pieces into the tin, skin side uppermost. Put the sorrel mixture onto the fish, pressing it firmly into place. Chill until needed.
7. Hang the tin from the 3rd runners in the roasting oven and bake for 20 minutes, then serve.

seafood cassoulet

To feed more people: Serve with baked potatoes to feed 6. Double the ingredients will feed up to 12

Serves 4

8 oz (225g) white fish
4 oz (110g) raw prawns
4 oz (110g) mixed shellfish
1 tbsp olive oil
2 onions
2 cloves garlic
1 tin (400g) butter beans
1 tin (400g) haricot beans
½ pint (300ml) fish stock
2 tbsp sun dried tomato purée
Salt and pepper
Chopped parsley to garnish

Oven:

Simmering oven, 130C, 250F,
Gas 1

Prepare in advance:

Make the cassoulet base and chill for up to 24 hours: reheat and add the fish

Prepare ahead:

Will keep warm in the simmering oven for half an hour, or longer before adding fish

Freeze:

Yes

1. Peel and chop the onion, crush the garlic. Open and drain the cans of beans.
2. Heat the oil in a heavy based pan, add the onion and garlic and cook until sizzling. Cover and transfer to the simmering oven for 15 minutes or so, to soften.
3. When the onions are soft, add the drained beans, fish stock, seasoning and tomato purée. Bring to the boil, then cover and return the pan to the simmering oven until you are ready to eat.
4. Just before serving, tip the fish and shellfish into the pan, stir well and leave to stand for 5 minutes, to cook the fish. Serve scattered with chopped parsley and a slice of crusty bread.

slow roasted dill salmon

To feed more people: A whole salmon, rather than just a fillet, will feed up to 12, but will be easier to serve if filleted before cooking

Serves 5–6

1 large whole salmon fillet
2 tbsp dill sauce
Black pepper

Dill Sauce:

2 tbsp chopped fresh dill
1 tbsp Dijon mustard
1 tbsp light muscovado sugar
1 tbsp double cream

Oven:

Simmering oven, 130C, 250F, Gas 1

Prepare in advance:

Make the sauce 24 hours in advance and warm gently on the back of the Aga

Prepare ahead:

Sauce will keep for an hour in a covered jug on the back of the Aga, the fish will keep warm in the simmering oven for half an hour

Freeze:

Uncooked fish

1. To make the sauce, mix all the ingredients together, or open a jar of prepared sauce!
2. Line the large roasting tin with Bake-O-Glide. Put the fish into the tin, skin side downwards, and smear the flesh with the dill sauce. Cover the tin tightly with foil.
3. Slide the tin into the simmering oven and bake for about an hour to an hour and a half.
4. Serve the fish with new potatoes, salad and more dill sauce.

Aga tip: If you want the fish to be cooked in a hurry, put the tin onto the 4th runners in the roasting oven for 20 minutes

haddock and spinach daal

To feed more people: Double the ingredients will feed up to 10, more if served as part of a curry buffet

Serves 4–5

8 oz (225g) fresh haddock
1 onion
1 clove garlic
½" piece fresh ginger
1 tbsp sunflower
1 tsp garam masala
4 oz (110g) red lentils
4 oz (110g) yellow split peas
1 pint (550ml) fish stock, water or water-mixed-with wine
Salt and pepper
8 oz (225g) spinach

Oven:

Simmering oven, 130C, 250F, Gas 1

Prepare in advance:

Cooked, cooled lentil mixture will keep in the fridge for up to 24 hours, reheat and then add the fish and spinach 5 minutes before serving

Prepare ahead:

Will keep warm in simmering or warming oven for up to an hour

Freeze:

Don't see why not!

1. Cut the haddock into ½"/1cm cubes. Set aside until needed.
2. Peel and chop the onion, crush the garlic and peel and grate the ginger. Heat the oil in a large pan and add onion, garlic and ginger and cook on the simmering plate for a minute, until sizzling.
3. Cover and put on the floor of the simmering oven for a further 10 minutes to soften.
4. Stir in the garam masala, lentils and split peas, then pour on the stock. Season, stir well and bring to the boil on the boiling plate. Cover and put in the simmering oven for 20 minutes.
5. Add the fish and spinach, stir well, cover and return to the simmering oven for a further 5 minutes.

spiced steamed halibut

To feed more people: Add two more pieces of fish to feed 6. Double all the ingredients will feed 8 but you will need a very large pan!

Serves 4

4 halibut steaks (about 4 oz/110g each) or any other firm white fish
1 onion
1 clove garlic
4 oz (110g) piece chorizo sausage
4 oz (110g) mushrooms
4 tomatoes
1 tbsp olive oil

1 tbsp chopped fresh parsley to finish

Oven:

Simmering oven, 130C, 250F, Gas 1

Prepare in advance:

Vegetable base will keep in fridge for up to 24 hours

Prepare ahead:

Will keep warm in simmering or warming oven

Freeze:

Yes – cook the vegetables, allow to cool and freeze with the raw fish on top. Defrost and reheat on the floor of the roasting oven for 15 minutes

1. Peel and chop the onion, crush the garlic, quarter the tomatoes and mushrooms and cut the chorizo into ½"/1cm chunks.
2. Heat the oil in a heavy pan that has a lid, and add the onion, garlic and chorizo. Stir the vegetables over the heat until sizzling, then cover the pan and transfer to the simmering oven for 10 minutes to soften.
3. When the onions are soft, move the pan to the simmering plate and add the mushrooms and tomatoes. Stir over the heat for a minute or two until they begin to release their juices, then lay the fish steaks on top.
4. Cover the pan and move it to the side of the Aga. The steam from the vegetables will cook the fish in about 5 minutes.
5. Serve with new potatoes and a scatting of chopped parsley to show you have made an effort!

orange salmon

To feed more people: Allow one salmon steak per person. Double the sauce will cover up to 12 pieces of salmon

Serves 4

4 salmon fillet pieces
2 tbsp orange juice
1 oz (25g) butter
Black pepper

For the sauce:

1 egg
Pinch mustard powder
Salt and pepper
Grated zest of an orange
1 tbsp orange juice
¼ pint (150ml) sunflower oil

Oven:

Roasting oven, 200C, 400F, Gas 6

Prepare in advance:

Make the sauce 24 hours in advance and warm gently on the back of the Aga

Prepare ahead:

Sauce, 1 hour in a covered jug on a cloth on the back of the Aga, the fish will keep warm in the simmering oven for half an hour

Freeze:

Uncooked fish only

1. Set the butter in a bowl on the back of the Aga to melt. Stand the jug of oil on the back of the Aga to warm up.
2. Sprinkle the fish with orange juice and a generous grind of pepper. Set aside for 15 minutes.
3. Line the small shallow baking tin with Bake-O-Glide. Put the fillets into the tin and brush with the melted butter. Hang the tin from the second runners in the roasting oven and bake for about 6 minutes. Set aside to keep warm.
4. For the sauce: Put the egg, seasoning, orange juice and rind into a blender. Whizz and then slowly pour in the oil until it thickens. Season and serve with the salmon.

chicken cacciatore

To feed more people: Double the ingredients will feed up to 10, three chickens and double the sauce will feed up to 15

Serves 4–5

1 chicken, jointed into 8 pieces or 8 chicken joints
2 oz (55g) plain flour
Salt and pepper
2 tbsp olive oil
2 onions
2 cloves garlic
2 tbsp sun dried tomato purée
1 lb (450g) ripe tomatoes or a tin of chopped tomatoes
1 red pepper
1 tbsp chopped fresh rosemary
½ pint (300ml) stock, mixed with some dry white wine if you have any to hand
1 tbsp red wine vinegar

Oven:

Floor of roasting oven then simmering oven, 130C, 250F, Gas 1

Prepare in advance:

Cooked, cooled chicken will keep in the fridge for 24 hours – it will improve in flavour!

Prepare ahead:

Will keep warm in the simmering or warming oven for an hour or so

Freeze:

Yes

1. Put the chicken pieces into a plastic bag and add the flour and seasonings. Shake to coat the meat in the flour.
2. Peel and chop the onion, crush the garlic, cut the tomatoes into quarters (or open the tin!) and slice the red pepper.
3. Heat the oil in a heavy pan on the simmering plate, add the meat and onions and transfer the pan to the floor of the roasting oven for 10 minutes to brown. Shake the pan to turn the meat, then return to the oven for a further 5 minutes.
4. Transfer the pan to the boiling plate and add the tomato purée, tomatoes, garlic, pepper and herbs. Stir, then pour in the liquid and stir until boiling.
5. Cover the pan and put into the simmering oven for at least 45 minutes or up to 2 hours.
6. If there is a lot of sauce, remove the lid and put the pan back onto the floor of the roasting oven to reduce for 10 minutes before serving.

mustard chicken

To feed more people: Allow one chicken breast per person. Double the topping will cover up to 10 pieces

Serves 4

4 boneless chicken breasts or 8 thighs
4 tbsp crème fraîche
1 clove garlic
2 tbsp Dijon mustard
Salt and pepper

Oven:

Roasting oven, 200C, 400F, Gas 6

Prepare in advance:

Leave the uncooked, covered chicken in the marinade in the fridge for up to 24 hours

Prepare ahead:

Will keep warm in the simmering or warming oven for an hour

Freeze:

Yes, but beware of reheating cooked chicken breasts as they can tend to be stringy, best to use thighs if freezing cooked

1. Line the small shallow baking tray with Bake-O-Glide.
2. Open out the chicken pieces and put into the tin.
3. Crush the garlic and put into a bowl with the crème fraîche, mustard and seasoning. Mix well, then spread this over the chicken pieces.
4. Leave to marinate for up to half an hour, or overnight in the fridge, or freeze uncooked.
5. Hang the tin from the 3rd runners in the roasting oven and bake for about 20 minutes until the sauce is bubbling and the chicken cooked through.
6. Serve with mashed potatoes and a green vegetable.

Ring the changes:

- Use pork fillet instead of the chicken, either whole and sliced once cooked, or cut into 1"/2cm slices before marinating and cooking
- Use a firm white fish such as monkfish instead of the chicken

allspice chicken stew

To feed more people: Double all of the ingredients will serve up to 9

Serves 4

2 tbsp olive oil
8 chicken thigh joints
1 onion
1 clove garlic
2 carrots
2 sticks celery
1 tbsp ground allspice
1 tbsp plain flour
½ pint (300ml) stock
1 tin (400g) haricot beans
1 tin (400g) butter beans
Chopped thyme to serve

Oven:

Simmering oven, 130C, 250F, Gas 1

Prepare in advance:

Cooked, cooled stew will keep in fridge for 24 hours

Prepare ahead:

Will keep warm in simmering oven for up to an hour

Freeze:

Yes

1. Peel and chop the onion, crush the garlic and cut the carrots and celery into even sized pieces. Open and drain the tins of beans.
2. Heat the oil in a heavy based pan on the simmering plate and add the chicken meat, onion, garlic, carrots and celery.
3. Shake the pan over the heat and once sizzling, transfer to the floor of the roasting oven to brown for about 5 minutes.
4. Shake the pan again, to turn the meat then return to the oven to brown on the other side.
5. Take the pan of browned meat and vegetables from the oven and put onto the boiling plate. Stir in the flour, allspice and stock, add the beans. Stir over the heat until boiling, then cover and move to the simmering oven for about 45 minutes.
6. Stir the stew and serve with a scattering of fresh chopped parsley.

chicken and mushroom pudding

To feed more people: Double the ingredients will fill a 4 pint/2 litre pudding bowl and will feed up to 14 – it will need an extra three hours in the oven

Serves 6

1½ lb (750g) boneless, skinless chicken thighs
8 oz (225g) button mushrooms
1 onion
½ pt (275ml) dry white wine
1 tbsp vegetable stock powder
1 tbsp plain flour
Salt and pepper

Pastry:

4 oz (110g) suet
8 oz (230g) self raising flour
About ¼ pint (150ml) water
2 tbsp plain flour

Oven:

Simmering oven, 130C, 250F, Gas 1

Prepare ahead:

Can sit for 12 hours in the simmering oven!

Freeze:

No

1. First make the pastry: sift the flour into a bowl and stir in the suet. Add cold water one tablespoon at a time, until you have a dough. Knead for 2 minutes until pliable, then roll out to approx 14"/35cm round. Cut out a quarter-sized slice and line a 2 pint/1 litre pudding basin with the large section. Re-roll the remaining quarter into an 8"/20cm round to make a lid for the pudding.
2. Cut the chicken into 1"/2½ cm cubes. Chop the onion. Halve the mushrooms. Put the plain flour and stock powder into a plastic bag with plenty of salt and pepper. Toss the meat, mushrooms and onion in the bag, then turn out into the lined pudding basin. Pour the wine over the meat.
3. Moisten the rim of the pastry lining the bowl and lay on the lid, pinching together the edges. Cover with cling film (or clip the lid onto the plastic bowl!).
4. Take a long piece of foil or cling film and fold lengthways into a long strip, which goes under the basin, to act as a handle. Fill a large saucepan with enough water to come about a third of the way up the sides of the bowl, and lower in the basin. Set the pan onto the boiling plate and bring to the boil. Cover with a lid and transfer to the simmering oven for at least 4 hours – or up to 6 hours.
5. To serve, lift out the pudding and wrap the bowl in a white linen napkin before bringing to the table.

chicken tikka masala

To feed more people: Double the ingredients will feed up to 9, or more if served as part of a curry buffet

Serves 4

1lb (450g) chicken thighs or a whole chicken, jointed and skinned
½ red chilli
2 cloves garlic
1" (2½ cm) fresh ginger
1 tbsp sunflower oil
2 tsp garam masala
¼ tsp smoked paprika
1 tsp sun dried tomato purée
1 onion
1 tin (400g) chopped tomatoes
¼ pint (150ml) yogurt
2 tbsp chopped coriander to finish

Oven:

Floor of roasting oven, simmering oven, 130C, 250F, Gas 1

Prepare in advance:

Cooked, cooled masala will keep in the fridge for 24 hours

Prepare ahead:

Will keep warm in the simmering oven for an extra hour or so

Freeze:

Yes

1. Remove the skin from the meat.
2. Peel the garlic and ginger.
3. Put the garlic, ginger, chilli, paprika, garam masala, tomato purée and oil into a blender and whizz to a paste. Tip into a plastic bag, add the chicken meat and seal the bag. Leave to marinate for an hour or chill overnight.
4. Peel and chop the onion. Open the tin of tomatoes.
5. Heat a heavy based pan and add the chicken and onion to the pan. Transfer the pan, uncovered, to the floor of the roasting oven to brown for 10 minutes, shaking the pan after 5 minutes.
6. Move the pan of browned meat to the simmering plate, stir in the tomatoes and yogurt. Bring to the boil, then cover and put into the simmering oven for 15 minutes. Serve with a scattering of chopped coriander and some Aga rice.

spiced chicken pilaf

To feed more people: Double the ingredients will feed up to 10

Serves 4–5

1½ lb (700g) boneless, skinless chicken thighs
1 tbsp olive oil
8 oz (225g) (½ pint in a measuring jug) long grain rice
¾ pint (425ml) stock
1 onion
1 clove garlic
10 cardamom pods
5 cloves
1 tsp ground cumin
½ tsp smoked paprika
4 oz (110g) frozen peas

Oven:

Simmering oven, 130C, 250F, Gas 1

Prepare in advance:

Cooked, cooled pilaf will keep in fridge for up to 24 hours

Prepare ahead:

Keep warm in the simmering oven for an hour

Freeze:

Yes, defrost and reheat in roasting oven for 25 minutes

1. Cut the chicken into ½"/1cm slices. Peel and chop the onion, crush the garlic.
2. Crush the cardamom and cloves in a pestle and mortar and remove the outer husk of the pods.
3. Heat the oil in a pan on the simmering plate and add the chicken, onion and garlic. Stir to mix then transfer the pan to the floor of the roasting oven to brown the meat for 5 minutes, shaking the pan once to turn the meat.
4. When the meat is brown, move the pan to the boiling plate and add the spices. Stir over the heat for a minute then add the rice and stock, stirring until it has boiled. Cover and transfer to the simmering oven for at least 20 minutes.
5. Once the rice is cooked and has absorbed all the stock, add the peas, re-cover the pan and return to the simmering oven for 5 minutes until the peas have thawed.
6. Serve hot.

clementine's coconut chicken

To feed more people: Double the ingredients will feed up to 9

Serves 4

- 4 chicken breasts
- 1 medium onion
- 2 cloves garlic
- 1 tbsp rapeseed oil
- 1 tsp ground coriander
- 1 tsp smoked paprika
- 1 tsp ground cumin
- 1 tsp garam masala
- ½ tsp ground ginger
- ¼ tsp salt
- 1 tin (340g) coconut milk

Oven:

Floor of roasting oven

Prepare in advance:

Cooked, cooled casserole will keep in the fridge for up to 24 hours

Prepare ahead:

Will keep warm in simmering or warming oven for an hour or so

Freeze:

Don't see why not!

1. Remove the skins from the chicken and cut into even sized pieces – the smaller the pieces, the faster the meat will cook.
2. Peel and chop the onion, crush the garlic. Measure out all the spices and salt into one bowl. Open the tin of coconut milk!
3. Heat the oil in a heavy based pan and add the chicken, onion and garlic. Shake over the heat for a minute then transfer the pan, uncovered, to the floor of the roasting oven to brown for about 7 minutes.
4. Move the pan to the simmering plate and add the spices. Stir over the heat, then add the coconut milk. Stir until boiling, then return to the floor of the roasting oven for 5 minutes to boil and thicken.
5. Serve with Aga rice and a green vegetable.

chicken layer bake

To feed more people: Double all the ingredients will feed 9 people. Double the other ingredients, but triple the meat, will feed 14 people; cook in the simmering oven for at least an hour and a half

Serves 4–5

- 4 chicken breasts
- 2 tbsp olive oil
- 2lb (900g) Maris Piper potatoes
- 2 medium onions
- 1 clove garlic
- ¾ pint (400ml) chicken stock
- ¼ pint (150ml) double cream
- 1 tbsp fresh tarragon
- Salt and pepper

Oven:

Floor of roasting oven, then simmering oven, 130C, 250F, Gas 1

Prepare in advance:

Cooked, cooled bake will keep in the fridge for 24 hours

Prepare ahead:

Will keep warm in simmering oven for an extra hour or so

Freeze:

Yes

1. Cut the meat into ½"/1cm slices. Peel and slice the onion and crush the garlic. Cut the potatoes into ½"/1cm slices.
2. Heat the oil in a heavy pan and add the chicken, garlic and onions. Stir over the heat until sizzling, then transfer to the floor of the roasting oven for 5 minutes to brown, shaking once or twice to turn the meat.
3. Lay a third of the sliced potatoes into a deep casserole. Spread half of the chicken and onion mixture over this, then another third of the potatoes. Put the rest of the chicken on top of the potatoes, then finish with the remaining potatoes.
4. Mix the stock and cream together, snip in the tarragon and season well.
5. Cover the casserole and put it onto the floor of the roasting oven for about 15 minutes to come to the boil, then transfer to the simmering oven for at least an hour.
6. Serve with a scattering of tarragon over the top and a green vegetable.

diamond jubilee chicken salad

To feed more people: Double all the ingredients will feed up to 12

Serves 5–6

3lb (1.5kg) chicken, cooked and cooled
½ lb (225g) cherries
4 spring onions
Bunch watercress

Dressing:

2 tbsp olive oil
1 tbsp cider vinegar
¼ pint (150ml) natural yogurt
Salt and pepper
Sprig fresh lavender or rosemary

Prepare ahead:

Cooked, cooled chicken will keep in the fridge for up to 24 hours
Finished salad will keep in the fridge for 4 hours

Freeze:

No

1. To cook the chicken – either 1 Put it into a casserole with a tight fitting lid and maybe a chopped onion, cover and put into the simmering oven for 3 hours or 2 Bring a large pan of water to the boil, put in the chicken, a chopped onion, some carrots and some parsley stalks, bring back to the boil then cover and put into the simmering oven for an hour. Take the chicken from the oven and allow to cool completely.
2. Remove the chicken meat from the bones and cut into ¾"/2cm pieces.
3. Remove the stones from the cherries by halving them and levering out the stones, or use a cherry stoner then halve the empty cherries.
4. Trim and slice the spring onions.
5. Chop the lavender or rosemary finely, then mix all the dressing ingredients together.
6. Stir together the chicken, cherries and spring onions, and dressing.
7. Arrange the watercress on a plate, pile the chicken mixture onto it and serve, garnished with some lavender or rosemary flowers.

Aga tip: Slow roasting the chicken in the simmering oven keeps it really moist and makes the pan lighter to lift into the simmering oven. Make sure it is covered tightly to contain the steam, or it will take all day to cook through

alix's spiced chicken with apricots

To feed more people: Double the ingredients will feed 12, more if part of a curry buffet

Serves 6

1 x 3lb (1.4kg) chicken, jointed or 6 chicken pieces
2 red chillies
1 stick cinnamon
1 tbsp cardamom pods
1 tsp ground cumin
10 whole cloves
2"/5cm piece fresh ginger
2 cloves garlic
2 large onions
4 oz (110g) dried apricots
2 tbsp sun dried tomato purée
½ pint (300ml) water
4 tbsp vegetable oil
1 tsp salt
2 tbsp white wine vinegar
1 tbsp caster sugar

Oven:

Simmering oven, 130C, 250F, Gas 1

Prepare in advance:

Cooked, cooled curry will keep in the fridge for up to 48 hours

Prepare ahead:

Keep warm in simmering or warming oven for an hour or so

Freeze:

Yes. Defrost then reheat for 30 minutes in the roasting oven

1. Crush the red chillies, ginger, garlic, cinnamon, cumin, cardamom and cloves into a mortar and pestle or mini-chopper.
2. Peel and slice the onions.
3. Put the chicken pieces into a plastic bag or large bowl and add about half of the spice mixture. Stir well to coat the meat in the spices. Set aside to marinate for at least an hour, or overnight.
4. Put the apricots into a pan with the water and tomato purée and set onto the back of the Aga to soften while the chicken marinates – this is fine to leave, covered, overnight.
5. Heat the oil in a large casserole on the simmering plate, add the chicken and onions and stir over the heat until sizzling. Transfer the pan to the floor of the roasting oven for about 10 minutes until the meat has browned, shaking it occasionally to turn the meat.
6. When the meat has browned, move the pan to the boiling plate and add all the remaining ingredients and stir. Bring to the boil, then cover and transfer to the simmering oven for an hour or so.
7. Serve with a scattering of chopped coriander and some Aga rice.

turkey curry

To feed more people: Double the ingredients will feed 8 or 9, or more if served with lots of rice, daal, poppadoms etc

Serves 4

1 lb (450g) turkey thigh meat
2 tbsp vegetable oil
1 large onion
2 cloves garlic
1 red chilli
1"/2cm piece fresh ginger
2 tsp garam masala
1 tsp black onion seeds
½ tsp salt
½ pint (300ml) stock
3 tsp natural yogurt
Chopped parsley or coriander to serve

Oven:

Simmering oven, 130C, 250F, Gas 1

Prepare in advance:

Cooked, cooled curry will keep in the fridge for up to 48 hours

Prepare ahead:

Keep warm in the simmering or warming oven for an hour or two

Freeze:

Yes

1. Cut the meat into 1"/2cm cubes.
2. Peel and chop the onion, crush the garlic and chop the chilli and ginger finely (or put it all into a processor and pulse until chopped).
3. Heat the oil in a heavy based pan and add the meat and vegetables. When sizzling, transfer the pan to the floor of the roasting oven to brown for 5 minutes, shaking the pan once.
4. Move the pan to the boiling plate, add the spices and salt and stir over the heat. Stir in the stock.
5. When the sauce is boiling, cover the pan and transfer to the simmering oven for an hour or two.
6. Just before serving, stir in the yogurt and scatter over some chopped parsley or coriander to show you have made an effort!

duck with blackcurrants

To feed more people: Allow six duck breasts for seven or eight people, as long as you carve them before they get to the table!

Serves 4

4 duck breasts
1 small tin (60g) blackcurrants in fruit juice
2 tsp cornflour
1 tsp stock powder
¼ pint (150ml) water
3 fl oz (75ml) double cream
Salt and pepper

Oven:

Floor of roasting oven and simmering plate

Prepare in advance:

Sauce will keep in the fridge for 24 hours, but meat is nicest eaten on the day it was cooked

Prepare ahead:

Will keep warm, before carving, in the simmering or warming oven for up to an hour

Freeze:

Yes, but it really is nicer eaten on the day it was cooked

1. Open the tin of blackcurrants and drain them, reserving the juices.
2. Score the skin of the duck breasts (to allow the fat to run away and to prevent it from curling as it is cooked).
3. Heat a ridged griddle pan in the roasting oven for 5 minutes, then put the breasts, skin side down, into the hot pan and put it onto the floor of the roasting oven. Griddle the breasts for 5–7 minutes each side, turning once. Move the cooked duck to a warm plate to rest for 5 minutes while you make the sauce.
4. Tip the blackcurrant juice and most of the water into a pan and bring to the boil and boil hard for two or three minutes to reduce it. Remove from the heat.
5. Mix the cornflour with the remaining water and add to the juice, together with the stock powder. Simmer until thickened, then remove from the heat and stir in the blackcurrants and cream. Season.
6. Carve the breasts into thin slices and arrange on plates. Pour over the sauce and serve.

chinese style duck parcels

To feed more people: Double the ingredients will feed up to 8, or many more if cooked half-sized and served as a canapé or starter

Serves 4

4 duck legs
4 tbsp hoisin sauce
1 orange
1 clove garlic
4 large or 8 small sheets filo pastry
2 tbsp sesame oil

Cucumber salsa:

½ cucumber
Bunch spring onions
1 tsp sesame oil
1 tsp rice vinegar

Oven:

Simmering oven, 130C, 250F, Gas 1 and roasting oven, 200C, 400F, Gas 1

Prepare in advance:

Uncooked parcels will keep in the fridge for 24 hours, wrapped in greaseproof not cling film, as that makes them go soggy!

Prepare ahead:

Keep warm for half an hour in the simmering oven

Freeze:

Uncooked parcels, cook from frozen for about 25 minutes

1. Put the duck legs into a saucepan, cover with a lid and put into the simmering oven for about 3 hours. (You can do this part up to 24 hours in advance and chill the duck meat once it has cooled.)
2. Remove the cooked duck legs from the oven and allow to cool for half an hour or so. Pour the duck fat from the pan into a jar and chill, for future roast potatoes!
3. Once the duck is cool enough to handle, peel off the skin and pull the meat away from the bones. Put the meat into a bowl with the hoisin sauce. Grate the rind of the orange onto the meat, crush the garlic and add. Stir together.
4. Lay a sheet of filo onto a work surface – if it is large, brush half with the sesame oil and fold in half to make a double thickness sheet, about 6"/15cm by 8"/20cm. If the filo is in smaller sheets, brush one with the oil and lay a second on top. Repeat until you have 4 prepared filo pieces.
5. Divide the duck mixture between the pastry sheets and roll up into parcels. Brush with more sesame oil.
6. Line a shallow baking tray with Bake-O-Glide and lay the parcels onto it. Hang the tin from the 3rd runners in the roasting oven and bake for about 15 minutes, until golden and crispy.
7. To make the salsa: Chop the cucumber into small dice and slice the spring onions finely. Toss in the oil and vinegar to mix thoroughly.
8. Serve the duck parcels with a spoonful of salsa.

duck with grapefruit

To feed more people: Two ducks will feed up to 10, or more with lots of roast potatoes

Serves 4

1 large-ish duck (4–5 lb, 2.5kg)
1 ruby grapefruit
3 tbsp grapefruit marmalade
¼ pint (150ml) stock
1 tbsp plain flour
Salt and pepper

Oven:

Simmering oven, 130C, 250F, Gas 1 and roasting oven, 200C, 400F, Gas 1

Prepare ahead:

Cooked duck will keep warm in simmering oven for an hour or so

Freeze:

Not really!

1. Take the duck from the fridge, remove the packaging and giblets, wipe dry and leave to come to room temperature for an hour.
2. Make some pâté from the liver and some stock from the giblets, or not.
3. Line a roasting tin with Bake-O-Glide and set the grill rack into it.
4. Grate the rind from the grapefruit and squeeze the juice. Cut the empty fruit skin into strips and push these into the cavity of the duck.
5. Set the duck onto the rack in the tin and cover tightly with foil. Put into the simmering oven and cook for about 4 hours.
6. When the duck is cooked, remove from the oven and lift into a clean roasting tin. Hang this tin, uncovered, from the second runners in the roasting oven for about 15 minutes for the skin to crisp and brown.
7. Strain the duck fat from the first tin and set aside for roast potatoes.
8. Mix the grapefruit juice and rind with the marmalade, flour and stock. Mix this into the remaining duck juices in the original tin and set it onto the floor of the roasting oven to boil and thicken.
9. Serve the duck with the sauce and all sorts of lovely crisp vegetables.

steak and stilton pudding

To feed more people: Double the ingredients will fill a 4 pint/2 litre pudding bowl and will feed up to 12. This will need an extra three hours in the simmering oven

Serves 6

1½ lb (750g) stewing beef
3 oz (85g) Stilton cheese
1 onion
½ pt (275ml) best bitter beer
1 tbsp vegetable stock powder
1 tbsp plain flour
Salt and pepper

Pastry:

4 oz (110g) suet
8 oz (230g) self raising flour
About ¼ pint (150ml) water
2 tbsp plain flour

Oven:

Simmering oven, 130C, 250F, Gas 1

Prepare ahead:

Can sit for 12 hours in the simmering oven!

Freeze:

No

1. First make the pastry: sift the flour into a bowl and stir in the suet. Add cold water one tablespoon at a time, until you have a dough. Knead for 2 minutes until pliable, then roll out to approx 14"/35cm round. Cut out a quarter-sized slice and line a 2pt/1 litre pudding basin with the large section. Re-roll the remaining quarter into an 8"/20cm round to make a lid for the pudding.
2. Cut the beef into 1"/2½cm cubes. Chop the onion. Crumble the Stilton. Put the plain flour and stock powder into a plastic bag with plenty of salt and pepper. Toss the meat, Stilton and onion in the bag, then turn out into the lined pudding basin. Pour the beer over the meat.
3. Moisten the rim of the pastry lining the bowl and lay on the lid, pinching together the edges. Cover with cling film (or clip the lid onto the plastic bowl!).
4. Take a long piece of foil or cling film and fold lengthways into a long strip, which goes under the basin, to act as a handle. Fill a large saucepan with enough water to come about a third of the way up the sides of the bowl, and lower in the basin. Set the pan onto the boiling plate and bring to the boil. Cover with a lid and transfer to the simmering oven for at least 4 hours – or up to 6 hours.
5. To serve, lift out the pudding and wrap the bowl in a white linen napkin before bringing to the table.

lasagne for charlotte's wedding

This looks like a really long and complicated recipe, but it feeds 15 and makes a brilliant main course for a big party

Serves 15

2½ lb (1kg) best minced beef
2 tbsp olive oil
3 onions
3 cloves garlic
3 sticks celery
8 oz (225g) smoked bacon
2 tins (2 x 4500g) chopped tomatoes
2 tbsp sun dried tomato purée
1 tbsp chopped oregano
½ tsp ground nutmeg
Salt and pepper
4 oz (110g) fresh spinach

1 packet (500g) no-cook dried lasagne

Sauce:

3 oz (85g) butter
3 oz (85g) plain flour
2 pints (1 litre) milk
1 large tub (500g) cottage cheese
Salt, pepper and nutmeg to season

1 lb (450g) leeks, trimmed
1 oz (25g) butter

1. Peel and chop the onion, crush the garlic, slice the celery and chop the bacon finely.
2. Put the mince, onion, garlic, celery and bacon into a large heavy pan and set onto the floor of the roasting oven to brown. Stir the pan after about 5 minutes, then return to the oven for a further 10 minutes to brown.
3. Move the pan to the boiling plate and add the tomatoes and tomato purée, oregano, nutmeg and seasoning. Stir together and bring to the boil. Cover and transfer the pan to the simmering oven for at least half an hour.
4. For the sauce, melt the butter in a pan on the simmering plate, stir in the flour and cook over the heat for a minute or two, then add the milk a little at a time, stirring all the time, until it boils and forms a thick white sauce. Season well and remove from the heat.
5. Using a processor, tip in the bread, Cheddar and nuts and whizz until well chopped and mixed. Tip into a bowl. Using the same, unwashed, processor bowl, slice the leeks thinly and tip them into a pan with their butter. Finally, before washing the processor bowl up, whizz the cottage cheese until smooth and stir it into the white sauce.
6. Heat the pan of leeks and butter on the simmering plate – lots of washing up in this recipe! Stir over the heat until sizzling, then cover and transfer to the simmering oven for about 15 minutes until softened.

Topping:

8 slices bread

4 oz (110g) Cheddar cheese

4 oz (110g) pecan nuts

Oven:

Roasting oven 200C, 400F, Gas 6 and simmering oven

Prepare in advance:

Assembled lasagne will keep for up to 48 hours in fridge

Prepare ahead:

Cooked lasagne will keep warm for an hour in the simmering oven

Freeze:

Uncooked lasagne

7. Take the pan of meat from the oven and allow to cool a little. Take two large ovenproof dishes – rectangular for ease of layering – and spoon a quarter of the meat into each.
8. Lay sheets of lasagne on top of the meat, then spread with just under a quarter of the sauce.
9. Add the cooked leeks to the remaining sauce on the pan and mix together.
10. Divide the spinach leaves between the two dishes, then pour the remaining meat onto the lasagne sheets. Shake to spread the meat evenly.
11. Lay more sheets of lasagne over the meat, then top with the leek sauce.
12. Finally, spread the bread, cheese and nut mixture over the top of the dishes and either chill, freeze or bake.
13. Set the grid shelf on the floor of the roasting oven and set the lasagnes onto it. Bake for about half an hour, until golden and bubbling.
14. Serve with garlic bread and a green salad.

sirloin steaks with blue cheese sauce

To feed more people: Double the quantity will feed 8, triple the quantity of meat but double the sauce will feed 12

Serves 4

4 sirloin steaks
1 onion
1 tbsp Dijon mustard
4 oz (110g) blue Stilton
4 oz (half a 200g pack) cream cheese
1 tbsp dry white vermouth

Prepare ahead:

No, serve as soon as it is ready

Freeze:

No

1. Put a deep sauté pan into the roasting oven to heat up for 5 minutes or so. Set the pack of cream cheese onto the back of the Aga to warm up and soften.
2. Transfer the pan to the boiling plate and put the steaks into it. Cook quickly, turning only once. When the steaks are cooked to your taste, remove from the pan and leave to rest. Approximate cooking times for thick steaks: rare: 3–4 minutes each side, medium: 5–6 minutes each side.
3. Slice the onion, crumble the Stilton.
4. Heat the oil in the pan, add the onion and put onto the floor of the roasting oven for about 5 minutes to brown.
5. Transfer the pan to the simmering plate and add the cream cheese, Stilton, mustard and vermouth. Stir over the heat until everything is melted, but do not allow to boil as it will separate.
6. Serve the steaks with the sauce poured over, with baked potatoes and lots of vegetables.

Aga tip: Heat the pan for the steaks in the roasting oven, saving the blast of heat of the boiling plate to sear and seal the meat quickly

meat loaf

To feed more people: Make two loaves in two loaf tins to feed up to 10

Serves 4

1½ lb (800g) best minced beef
1 onion
1 clove garlic
1 tbsp mixed dried herbs
1 tbsp smoked paprika
1 tbsp sun dried tomato purée
2 slices bread
1 egg
Salt and pepper

Oven:

Baking oven, 180C, 350F, Gas 4

Prepare in advance:

Eat it hot on the day you make it, eat it cold the next day!

Prepare ahead:

Will keep warm for up to an hour in the simmering or warming oven

Freeze:

Yes, uncooked

1. Line a 2lb/1kg loaf tin with Bake-O-Glide.
2. Put all the ingredients into a processor and whizz until mixed.
3. Tip the mixture into the prepared tin and cover with foil.
4. 2 oven Aga: Set the tin into a deep roasting tin and slide it onto the 4th runners in the roasting oven, with the plain shelf on the 2nd runners above. Bake for about 45 minutes, then move the tin to the simmering oven for about another 45 minutes – don't forget to remove the plain shelf from the roasting oven!
5. 3 and 4 oven Aga: Put the grid shelf on the floor of the baking oven and put the loaf tin onto it. Bake for about 1¼ hours.
6. When the loaf is cooked, remove from the oven and tip away any excess fat from the tin. Turn out the loaf and serve in slices, either hot with tomato sauce or mustard sauce and lots of mashed potato, or cold with salad and mustard mayonnaise.

Quick mustard sauce: Set a tub of cream cheese on the back of the Aga to soften. Just before serving, add a tablespoon of grainy mustard and a couple of tablespoons of milk. Stir and serve

beef with prunes

To feed more people: Double the ingredients will feed up to 9, three times will spread round 14, more if you add a couple of handfuls of lentils at the same time as the beer etc

Serves 4

- 1½ lb (700g) stewing steak
- 1 large onion
- 1 clove garlic
- 1 pint (550ml) best bitter beer
- 2 tbsp redcurrant or quince jelly
- 8 oz (225g) ready to eat prunes
- Salt and pepper
- 1 tbsp Worcester sauce
- 2 tbsp oil for frying
- 2 tbsp plain flour
- 4 oz (110g) mushrooms
- 1 tbsp chopped parsley

Oven:

Floor of roasting oven, simmering oven, 130C, 250F, Gas 1

Prepare in advance:

Cooked, cooled stew will keep in the fridge for up to 48 hours

Prepare ahead:

Stew will keep warm in the simmering or warming oven for an additional hour or two

Freeze:

Yes

1. Cut the meat into 1"/2½cm cubes. Chop the onion. Peel and crush the garlic. Quarter the prunes.
2. Put the flour, salt and pepper into a plastic bag and add the meat. Toss to coat evenly.
3. Heat the oil in a casserole pan and add the meat, onion and garlic. Transfer the pan to the floor of the roasting oven for 5 minutes to brown. Shake the pan and return it to the floor of the oven for a further 5 minutes.
4. Transfer the pan to the boiling plate and add the prunes, beer, jelly and Worcester sauce and bring to the boil, stirring. Cover and move to the simmering oven for about 2 hours.
5. Wipe over the mushrooms and quarter if large. Stir into the casserole and return to the oven for another 30 minutes.
6. Serve sprinkled with parsley, with mashed potato and a green vegetable.

Aga tip: Casseroles and stews improve in flavour if cooked one day, cooled and chilled overnight then reheated on the day they are eaten. Reheat in the roasting oven for half an hour until boiling, then move to the simmering oven until ready to eat

venison pie

To feed more people: Double the ingredients will feed up to 9, three times will spread round 14, more if you add a couple of handfuls of lentils or butter beans at the same time as the stock etc

Serves 4

1½ lb (700g) diced venison steak
1 large onion
1 clove garlic
½ pint (300ml) good stock
2 tbsp redcurrant or quince jelly
8 oz (230g) mushrooms
Salt and pepper
1 tbsp oil for frying
1 tbsp plain flour
Sprig of lavender or rosemary

1 packet (375g) ready rolled puff pastry
1 egg

Oven:

Floor of roasting oven, simmering oven, 130C, 250F, Gas 1 and roasting oven, 200C, 400F, Gas 6

Prepare in advance:

Cooked, cooled stew will keep in the fridge for up to 48 hours, with or without the uncooked pastry on top

Prepare ahead:

Pie will keep warm in the simmering or warming oven for an additional hour or two

Freeze:

Yes, with or without the uncooked pastry on top. Defrost and bake for an extra 5 minutes to reheat fully

1. Cut the meat into 1"/2½cm cubes. Chop the onion. Peel and crush the garlic. Quarter the mushrooms.
2. Put the flour, salt and pepper into a plastic bag and add the meat. Toss to coat evenly.
3. Heat the oil in a casserole pan and add the meat, onion and garlic. Transfer the pan to the floor of the roasting oven for 5 minutes to brown. Shake the pan and return it to the floor of the oven for a further 5 minutes.
4. Transfer the pan to the boiling plate and add the stock, mushrooms, jelly, lavender and seasoning then bring to the boil, stirring. Cover and move to the simmering oven for about 2 hours.
5. Remove from the oven and eat as a casserole, or continue for a pie …
6. Leave the meat to cool completely then tip into a pie dish. Don't forget to take out the sprig of lavender or rosemary now that it has done its job to flavour the sauce. (Mum! There's a stick in my stew again.)
7. Unroll the pastry and cut to fit the top of dish. Use the trimmings to make strips of pastry. Brush the edge of the dish with beaten egg, then lay on the strips of pastry. Brush with more beaten egg, then put the pastry sheet on top of the dish. Trim and press down the edges with a fork to create a pretty pattern. Brush the top with beaten egg.
8. Set the grid shelf on the floor of the roasting oven and put the pie dish into it. Bake for about 25 minutes until the pastry is puffed up and golden and the meat bubbling underneath.
9. Serve sprinkled with parsley, with mashed potato and a green vegetable.

mystery lamb casserole

To feed more people: Add an extra spoonful or two of lentils to stretch the stew for another person, or double all the ingredients to feed 8 or 9

Serves 4

1 lb (450g) lamb neck fillet
1 onion
1 clove garlic
1 tbsp olive oil
2 carrots
1 leek
1 tsp anchovy paste
½ pint (300ml) stock
2 tbsp dry white vermouth
3 tbsp red lentils

Oven:

Simmering oven, 130C, 250F, Gas 1

Prepare in advance:

Cooked cooled casserole will keep in fridge for 24 hours

Prepare ahead:

Keep warm in simmering oven for an extra hour or so

Freeze:

Yes

1. Cut the lamb into even sized pieces. Peel and chop the onion, crush the garlic and trim and slice the leek and carrots.
2. Heat the olive oil in a heavy based pan on the simmering plate and add the meat and vegetables. Shake over the heat then transfer the pan to the floor of the roasting oven for 10 minutes to brown, shaking the pan occasionally.
3. Move the pan to the boiling plate and stir in the anchovy paste. Add the stock, lentils and vermouth, stirring all the time until it is boiling, then cover and put into the simmering oven for an hour or so.
4. Serve with lots of mashed potato to soak up the sauce.

lamb and coconut pilaf

To feed more people: Double the ingredients will feed up to 12

Serves 6

- 1 tbsp olive oil
- 1½ lb (700g) lamb neck fillet
- 2 onions
- 2 cloves garlic
- 2 tbsp garam masala
- 1 green chilli
- 1 can (400g) coconut milk
- ¾ pint (450ml) in a jug, rice
- ¼ pint (150ml) stock
- Salt and pepper
- 1 mango
- 1 tbsp flaked almonds
- 1 tbsp pine nuts
- Fresh coriander to serve

Oven:

Floor of roasting oven then simmering oven, 130C, 250F, Gas 1

Prepare in advance:

Cooked, cooled pilaf will keep in the fridge for 24 hours

Prepare ahead:

Will keep warm in simmering or warming oven for an additional hour or so

Freeze:

Yes

1. Cut the lamb into chunks.
2. Peel and chop the onions and chilli, crush the garlic. Peel and chop the mango.
3. Heat the oil in a heavy based pan and add the onions, garlic and lamb. Stir over the heat until sizzling then transfer the pan to the floor of the roasting oven for 5–10 minutes to brown, shaking the pan once to turn the meat.
4. Transfer the pan to the boiling plate and add the garam masala and chilli. Stir over the heat, then add the coconut milk and stock. Season and bring to the boil, then cover and move the pan to the simmering oven for 15–150 minutes.
5. Just before serving, stir in the mango, almonds and pine nuts and scatter over a spoonful of chopped coriander.

tomato and cardamom lamb casserole

To feed more people: Add a spoonful or two of lentils to stretch the stew for another person, or double all the ingredients to feed 8 or 9

Serves 4

1 lb (450g) lamb neck fillet
1 onion
1 clove garlic
1 tbsp olive oil
4 medium tomatoes
12 cardamom pods
1 can (400g) butter beans
½ pint (300ml) stock
1 tbsp plain flour
2 tbsp red wine

Oven:

Simmering oven, 130C, 250F, Gas 1

Prepare in advance:

Cooked, cooled casserole will keep in fridge for 24 hours

Prepare ahead:

Keep warm in simmering oven for an extra hour or so

Freeze:

Yes

1. Cut the lamb into even sized pieces. Peel and chop the onion, crush the garlic, quarter the tomatoes and crush the cardamom pods and remove the seeds. Open the can of beans and drain them.
2. Heat the olive oil in a heavy based pan on the simmering plate and add the meat, onion and garlic. Shake over the heat then transfer the pan to the floor of the roasting oven for 10 minutes to brown, shaking the pan occasionally.
3. Move the pan to the boiling plate and stir in the flour, tomatoes, beans and cardamom seeds. Add the stock and wine, stirring all the time until it is boiling, then cover and put into the simmering oven for an hour or so.
4. Serve with lots of mashed potato to soak up the sauce.

mustard roasted lamb

To feed more people: A larger joint will feed more people – double all the sauce ingredients will feed 10 people. Serve with lots of extra vegetables to stretch the meat further!

Serves 4–6

3–4 lb (1.5–2kg) leg of lamb

2 tbsp Dijon mustard

Glass of red wine

3 tbsp redcurrant jelly

Small pot (150ml) crème fraîche

Salt and pepper

Oven:

Roasting oven, 200C, 400F, Gas 6

Prepare ahead:

Lamb joint will keep warm in the simmering oven for an extra hour or so, but it will continue to cook a little. Keep the sauce warm in a jug on the back of the Aga.

Freeze:

No

1. Line the small roasting tin with Bake-O-Glide.
2. Smear the mustard all over the lamb and put it into the tin. Hang the tin from the 3rd runners in the roasting oven and roast for an hour.
3. When the lamb is cooked, remove it from the tin and put onto a plate and leave to rest in the simmering or warming oven while you make the sauce.
4. Tip away any excess fat in the tin, leaving about 2 tbsp, plus any crunchy bits from the lamb.
5. Add the wine, redcurrant jelly and crème fraîche to the tin, season and mix well.
6. Set the tin onto the floor of the roasting oven for 5 minutes until boiling and thickened.
7. Serve the lamb in slices, with a little sauce poured over. Not forgetting the roast potatoes, of course!

spiced lamb with apricots

To feed more people: Double all the ingredients will feed 8 people. Double the other ingredients, but triple the meat, will feed 12 people, but will need at least an hour in the simmering oven

Serves 4

- 2 lb (1kg) lamb neck fillet
- 2 onions
- 2 cloves garlic
- 2 tbsp vegetable oil
- 1 tsp ground cumin
- 1 tsp ground turmeric
- 2 tsp smoked paprika
- 2 oz (55g) sultanas
- 1 tbsp redcurrant jelly
- 1 pint (550ml) stock
- 1 tin (400g) cherry tomatoes
- 12 oz (375g) ready to eat dried apricots

Oven:

Simmering oven, 130C, 250F, Gas 1

Prepare in advance:

Cooked, cooled lamb will keep in fridge for 24 hours

Prepare ahead:

Will keep warm in simmering oven for an extra hour

Freeze:

Yes

1. Peel and slice the onions, peel and crush the garlic. Cut the meat into ½"/1cm slices. Slice the apricots.
2. Heat the oil in a heavy casserole and add the meat, garlic and onions. Transfer to the floor of the roasting oven to brown for 5 minutes, then shake and return to the oven for a further 5 minutes.
3. Move the pan to the boiling plate and add ground spices and fry again for a minute.
4. Add the sultanas, jelly, stock, apricots and tomatoes, stir and bring to the boil.
5. Cover and put into the simmering oven for 45 minutes.
6. Serve with couscous or rice.

classic moussaka

To feed more people: Double the ingredients will fill the large roasting tin and should feed more than 12

Serves 6

1½ lb (700g) lamb mince
1 onion
2 cloves garlic
1 tins (400g) chopped tomatoes
½ tsp ground cinnamon
½ tsp ground allspice
1 tsp sun dried tomato purée
2 bay leaves
Sprig fresh thyme
¼ pint (150ml) red wine
Salt and pepper
2 large aubergines

Topping:

2 oz (55g) butter
2 oz (55g) plain flour
1 pint (550ml) milk
3 oz (85g) grated Gruyère
1 egg
2 oz (55g) Parmesan

Oven:

Roasting oven, 200C, 400F, Gas 6 and simmering oven, 130C, 250F, Gas 1

Prepare in advance:

Assembled moussaka will keep in the fridge for up to 24 hours

Prepare ahead:

Will keep warm in the simmering oven for up to an hour

Freeze:

Yes, assembled but uncooked

1. Peel and chop the onion, crush the garlic.
2. Set the milk for the topping in a jug on the back of the Aga to warm up and put the butter in a pan on the back of the Aga to melt.
3. Put the lamb mince, onion and garlic into a sauté pan and set it into the boiling plate until it sizzles. Move the pan to the floor of the roasting oven for 5–10 minutes for the meat to brown.
4. When the meat has browned, move the pan to the boiling plate and stir in the spices, tomato purée, tin of tomatoes and the herbs. Season and bring to the boil, then cover and move to the simmering oven for about half an hour.
5. Trim and slice the aubergines. Heat a griddle pan on the boiling plate and add the slices of aubergine – you might need to do this in two or three batches. Cook for about 3 minutes on each side, turning once. Put them onto a cooling rack to cool.
6. Make the topping: Stir the flour into the melted butter in the pan, then add the milk. Set the pan onto the simmering plate and bring to the boil, stirring all the time. When the sauce has boiled, remove from the heat and beat in the egg and Gruyère cheese.
7. Tip the cooked mince into the small roasting tin. Lay the slices of cooked aubergine onto the mince, then pour the cheese sauce over. Grate the Parmesan on the top, then bake in the centre of the roasting oven for about 40 minutes until golden brown and bubbling.

kate's orange and cumin pork fillet

To feed more people: Double the ingredients will feed up to 10, triple the meat but double the sauce will feed up to 16

Serves 4–5

1½ lb (700g) pork fillet
3 cloves garlic
3 tbsp ground cumin
2 oranges
2 tbsp fresh sage
2 tbsp light muscovado sugar
1 tbsp olive oil

Oven:

Roasting oven, 200C, 400F, Gas 6

Prepare in advance:

Let the meat sit in its marinade for 24 hours in the fridge

Prepare ahead:

Will keep warm in the simmering or warming oven for up to an hour

Freeze:

Yes, raw meat in its marinade

1. Put the pork fillets into a large ovenproof dish.
2. Grate the rind of the oranges and squeeze the juice. Crush the garlic. Chop the oregano.
3. Mix together the orange rind, cumin and garlic, and add the orange juice, sugar, sage and oil.
4. Tip the marinade over the pork, cover and leave to soak up the flavours for at least an hour, or all day.
5. Remove the cover and put the dish into the roasting oven (sit it on the grid shelf on the 4th runners) and bake for about 35 minutes until browned and delicious.
6. Let the meat stand for 5 minutes before serving in slices, with the juices poured over.

bacon and chicken pie

Serves 4

12 oz (350g) plain flour
4 oz (110g) lard or butter
8 tbsp water
Salt and pepper

1 lb (450g) chicken thigh meat, boned and skinless
8 oz (225g) bacon pieces
1 tsp chicken stock powder
Salt and pepper

1 egg, beaten

½ pint (300ml) good home made chicken stock

Oven:

Baking oven, 180C, 375F, Gas 4, then simmering oven, 130C, 250F, Gas 1

Prepare in advance:

Cooked, cooled pie will keep in the fridge for 48 hours

Freeze:

Yes

1. Put the lard or butter and water into a pan and set on the simmering plate to melt together. Bring to the boil, then tip in the flour and beat to a dough.
2. Grease a 6"/15cm cake tin and put in about two thirds of the pastry. Spread this out to cover the base and sides of the tin. Leave to cool, wrapping the remaining third of the pastry in clingfilm until needed.
3. Chop the chicken thighs and bacon into small dice. Mix with the stock powder and seasoning, and pile into the tin. Press down so that it all fits in.
4. Roll out the remaining pastry to make a lid for the pie – stick it on with some water and press down on the edges to seal, make a hole in the top for steam to escape, brush with beaten egg, then bake the pie.
5. 3 and 4 oven Aga: put the grid shelf on the floor of the baking oven and set the tin onto it. Bake for about 1½ hours until well browned, then transfer to the simmering oven for a further hour to finish cooking.
6. 2 oven Aga: Set the tin into the large roasting tin and hang from the 4th runners in the roasting oven, and slide the plain shelf onto the 2nd runners. Bake for about 50 minutes until well browned, then transfer the pie to the simmering oven for a further hour and a half to continue cooking without browning any more.
7. Take the pie from the oven and allow to cool a little. While it is cooling, bring the stock to boiling point. Using a funnel, pour the stock into the hole in the centre of the pie to fill any gaps left when the meat shrank as it cooked. Chill for at least 4 hours for the stock to set and become a jelly.
8. Serve the pie cold, but not straight from the fridge.

seriously slow aromatic pork shoulder

To feed more people: Double all of the ingredients will serve up to 15, but a larger joint will take an extra couple of hours to cook

Serves 8

5 lb /2.5kg shoulder of pork
3 onions
1 clove garlic
1 tbsp cardamom seeds (removed from their pods)
Good slurp of dry white vermouth
¼ pint (150ml) stock
2 tbsp cold water
1 tbsp cornflour

Oven:

Simmering oven, 130C, 250F, Gas 1

Prepare in advance:

Will keep in the fridge for up to 24 hours

Prepare ahead:

Will sit happily in the simmering oven for an extra hour or so!

Freeze:

Yes

1. Peel and slice the onions and crush the garlic.
2. Grind the cardamom seeds with the salt and pepper, then rub this powder into the pork skin.
3. Line a roasting tin with Bake-O-Glide.
4. Tip the onions and garlic into the tin and set the pork joint on top of the vegetables.
5. Pour the vermouth and stock into the tin, then cover with foil and put into the simmering oven for about 5 hours until the meat is meltingly tender and falling apart.
6. Remove from the oven, take the skin off and set the joint aside to rest.
7. Put the skin into a clean roasting tin. Hang the tin from the 2nd runners in the roasting oven for about 15 minutes to crisp up and brown.
8. For the sauce, mix the water with the cornflour and stir this into the onions and juices from the joint. Set the tin onto the floor of the roasting oven for 5 minutes until the sauce is bubbling and thickened.
9. Serve the pork with its crackling, sauce and some layered potatoes and a green vegetable.

bean and sausage casserole

To feed more people: Double the ingredients will feed up to 9

Serves 4

450g (1 lb) good-quality pork sausages
2 tbsp olive oil
1 medium onion, finely sliced
2 cloves garlic, crushed
3 rashers smoked back bacon, rind removed and cut into strips
4 tbsp dry white vermouth
1 tin (400g) canellini beans, drained
1 tin (400g) butter beans, drained
1 tin (400g) chopped tomatoes
Salt and pepper
1 tbsp chopped fresh basil

Oven:

Roasting oven, 200C, 400F, Gas 6 and simmering oven, 130C, 250F, Gas 1

Prepare in advance:

Cooked, cooled casserole will keep in the fridge for up to 48 hours

Prepare ahead:

Will keep warm in simmering oven for an hour or more

Freeze:

Yes

1 Separate and slice the sausages into 1"/2cm rounds and place the oil in a heavy-based casserole. Heat on a low heat and add the sausages, turning so that they become coated with the oil.
2 Transfer the pan to the floor of the roasting oven and allow the sausages to cook for 10 minutes, shaking occasionally, until golden brown. Pour off any excess fat, leaving about a tablespoonful. Add the onion, garlic and bacon and mix well, then return to the floor of the oven for 10 minutes to brown.
3 Set the pan onto the simmering plate and stir in the drained beans, tin of tomatoes, vermouth and season with salt and pepper to taste. Bring to the boil, then cover and put into the simmering oven for about half an hour.
4 Stir in the basil and serve with mashed potato, baked potatoes or just fresh bread.

hoisin glazed ham

To feed more people: A larger (or smaller) ham takes proportionately longer (or shorter!) to cook

Serves 10–12

5lb (2½ kg) piece ham

3 tbsp hoisin sauce from a bottle

1 orange, sliced

Oven:

Simmering oven, 130C, 250F, Gas 1, then roasting oven, 200C, 400F, Gas 6

Prepare in advance:

Cooked, cooled ham will keep in the fridge for 48 hours

Prepare ahead:

Will keep warm in the simmering or warming oven for an hour or so

Freeze:

No

1. Put the ham into a large pan. Cover with a well-fitting lid and put the pan into the simmering oven.
2. Cook the ham for 45 minutes per pound, or 90 minutes per kilo.
3. Line the large roasting tin with Bake-O-Glide.
4. When the ham is cooked, remove it from the pan. Using a sharp knife, peel away the skin, leaving a thin covering of fat. Score the fat with diagonal lines, then smear the hoisin sauce over the fat and the exposed ends of the joint.
5. Set the joint into the roasting tin and hang this from the 4th runners in the roasting oven. Cook for about 15 minutes, until the glaze is golden brown and bubbling.
6. Decorate with slices of fresh orange and serve.

hungarian pork

To feed more people: Double the ingredients will serve up to 10

Serves 4–5

2 pork fillets, about 1½ lb (700g)
1 oz (25g) butter
1 medium onion
2 tsp smoked paprika
2 tsp plain flour
¼ pint (150ml) medium sherry
3 oz (85g) mushrooms
¼ pint (150ml) stock
3 fl oz (75ml) double cream

Oven:

Floor of roasting oven, simmering oven, 130C, 250F, Gas 1

Prepare in advance:

Cooked, cooled casserole will keep in the fridge for 24 hours

Prepare ahead:

Will keep warm in simmering or warming oven for an hour or so

Freeze:

Yes

1. Chop the onions. Cut the fillets into ½"/1cm slices across the grain of the meat.
2. Melt the butter in a heavy pan and add the pork and onions. Transfer to the floor of the roasting oven to brown for 5 minutes.
3. Move the pan to the boiling plate and add the paprika and cook for a minute. Stir in the flour, then the sherry and stock.
4. Bring to the boil, cover and move to the simmering oven for at least 30 minutes.
5. Add the mushrooms and return to the simmering oven for a further 5 minutes.
6. To serve, stir in the cream and garnish with chopped parsley.

pork hotpot

To feed more people: Double all the ingredients will feed 9 people. Double the other ingredients, but triple the meat, will feed 14 people; cook in the simmering oven for at least an hour

Serves 4

- 1 lb (450g) pork fillet
- 2 tbsp olive oil
- 1 medium onion
- 1 clove garlic
- 8 oz (225g) button mushrooms
- ¼ pint (150ml) apple juice
- 2 tbsp dark rum
- ¼ pint (150ml) stock
- 1 tbsp Dijon mustard
- 1 tbsp plain flour
- Handful fresh parsley, chopped

Oven:

Floor of roasting oven, then simmering oven, 130C, 250F, Gas 1

Prepare in advance:

Cooked, cooled hotpot will keep in the fridge for 24 hours

Prepare ahead:

Will keep warm in simmering oven for an extra hour or so

Freeze:

Yes

1. Cut the meat into 1"/2cm cubes. Peel and slice the onion and crush the garlic. Quarter the mushrooms.
2. Heat the oil in a heavy pan and add the meat, garlic and onions. Stir over the heat until sizzling, then transfer to the floor of the roasting oven for 10 minutes to brown, shaking once or twice to turn the meat.
3. Tip in the mushrooms, mustard, flour, rum, apple juice and stock, stirring well to blend. Bring to the boil, then cover and put into the simmering oven for 45 minutes.
4. To finish, scatter over the parsley and serve with mashed potato.

pork wellington

To feed more people: Either, using double the ingredients, cook a second fillet in another piece of pastry, or cook two fillets and wrap them into a parcel together with two pieces of pastry, to serve up to 10

Serves 4

Whole fillet of pork (about 1lb, 500g)
2 tbsp olive oil
2 cloves garlic
Pack (375g) ready rolled puff pastry
1 pack (200g) mushroom paté
1 egg, beaten

1 tbsp plain flour
½ pint (300ml) stock
1 tbsp apple sauce
Salt and pepper

Oven:
Roasting oven, 200C, 400F, Gas 6

Prepare in advance:
24 hours, before cooking the pastry

Prepare ahead:
Will keep warm for up to an hour

Freeze:
Yes, before cooking the pastry

1. Smear the oil over the meat and crush the garlic and rub it over the oily meat. Grind on some salt and pepper then put into the large roasting tin, lined with Bake-O-Glide and hang from the second set of runners in the roasting oven for 15 minutes.
2. Once the meat is browned, remove from the oven and allow to cool completely. Reserve the juices in the roasting tin for the gravy.
3. Lay a sheet of Bake-O-Glide on the plain shelf. Unroll the puff pastry onto it. Brush the edges with beaten egg. Lay the cold meat onto the pastry.
4. Spread the paté over the meat. Fold the edges of the pastry around the meat and roll up like a giant sausage roll.
5. Brush with beaten egg to glaze. Make pretty shapes (leaves, letters, etc) with any pastry trimmings and decorate the Wellington, then glaze the decorations with more egg.
6. Set the plain shelf onto the floor of the roasting oven and bake for about 20 minutes until puffed up and golden.
7. To make the gravy: add the flour to the juices in the roasting tin and stir well, pour on the stock and apple sauce. Season and mix well. Put the tin onto the floor of the roasting oven for about 5 minutes until the gravy is boiling and thickened.

Whether serving hot, tepid or cold, it is important to eat the Wellington on the day that it has been cooked, as the pastry really does not do justice to the meat once it has been cooked and refrigerated

WELLINGTON

carnation chocolate pudding

To feed more people: Serve in smaller containers to stretch round 8, or double the quantity will feed 16

Serves 6

2 x large (150g each) bars plain chocolate

1 tin (400g) condensed milk

½ pint (300ml) double cream

1 tin condensed caramel

1 tsp sea salt

Oven:

Back of Aga

Prepare in advance:

Will keep in the fridge for 24 hours

Freeze:

Don't see why not, but maybe not in your most precious crystal wine glasses!

1. Break up the bars of chocolate and set in a bowl on the back of the Aga to melt. Put the unopened tin of condensed milk onto the back of the Aga to warm up. Take the cream from the fridge and set beside the Aga.
2. Open the can of caramel and stir in the salt.
3. Spoon the caramel into the bottom of six (or eight) wine glasses or ramekins.
4. Mix together the melted chocolate, condensed milk, and stir in the warmed cream. Beat until smooth, then pour over the salted caramel in the glasses.
5. Chill for at least 4 hours or overnight until set, then serve.

Aga tip: Melting chocolate on the back of the Aga means that it will never overheat or separate into grains

chestnut roulade

To feed more people: Roll the roulade along its long side to make a smaller, longer roll and cut into 10 slices, or make two roulades to cut into 16 slices

Serves 8

6 eggs

6 oz (175g) light soft brown sugar

1 packet (500g) prepared cooked chestnuts

½ pint (300ml) double cream

3½ oz pack (100g) white chocolate drops

Grated rind of an orange

Oven:

Baking oven, 170C, 370F, Gas 4

Prepare in advance:

Will keep in the fridge for up to 24 hours

Freeze:

Yes

1. Line the large roasting tin with Bake-O-Glide. Put the chocolate drops in a bowl on the back of the Aga to melt.
2. Tip the packet of chestnuts into a processor and whizz to a powder.
3. Whisk the eggs and sugar until very thick.
4. Fold the chestnuts into the egg mixture, then spread over the tin.
5. 2 oven Aga: Hang the tin from the 4th, lowest, runners in the roasting oven, with the plain shelf on the 2nd runners above. Bake for about 20 minutes until puffed up and golden.
6. 3 and 4 oven Aga: Hang the tin from the 3rd runners in the baking oven and bake for about 25 minutes until puffed up and golden.
7. When the cake is cooked, tip it out onto a clean tea towel and remove the Bake-O-Glide. Roll the roulade up in the towel and leave to cool completely.
8. To fill the cake, unroll the tea towel.
9. Whip the cream for the filling, add the melted chocolate and grate in the orange rind (and maybe add a spoonful of Cointreau?); spread this over the cake, then roll up again and chill for an hour until firm.

apricot cheesecake

To feed more people: Double all of the ingredients will fill a 10"/25cm tin and will serve up to 15

Serves 4

8 oz (225g) Hob Nob biscuits
2 oz (55g) butter
1 oz (25g) light muscovado sugar

12 oz (675g) fresh apricots
1 tub (200g) mascarpone cheese
½ pint (150ml) natural set yogurt
4 oz caster sugar
2 eggs

Oven:

Roasting oven, 200C, 400F, Gas 6

Prepare in advance:

Will keep in the fridge for up to 24 hours

Freeze:

Yes

1. Put the butter in a bowl on the back of the Aga to melt, or melt it in a pan on the simmering plate. Set the tub of mascarpone on the back of the Aga to soften.
2. Crush the biscuits and add them, with the sugar, to the melted butter.
3. Line a 9"/23cm loose based tin with Bake-O-Glide.
4. Tip the biscuit mix into the tin and press across the base and up the sides of the tin, then chill or freeze until needed.
5. Mix together the soft mascarpone, yogurt, sugar and eggs. Spread this over the prepared biscuit base.
6. Halve the apricots, remove the stones and arrange the halves on top of the cheese mixture. Sprinkle with icing sugar.
7. Put the grid shelf onto the floor of the roasting oven and put the tin onto it. Bake for 15–20 minutes until the sugar has browned and the apricots softened. Serve tepid.

cardamom cream rice

To feed more people: Double the ingredients will feed up to 9, but will need an extra half an hour in the simmering oven

Serves 4

2 oz (55g) pudding rice
1 oz (25g) sugar
1 tbsp cardamom seeds – removed from their green pods
1 pint (550ml) creamy milk
1 egg
2 tbsp water
3 tsp gelatine powder
½ pint (150ml) whipping cream

Oven:

Simmering oven, 130C, 250F, Gas 1

Prepare in advance:

Will keep in the fridge for up to 24 hours

Freeze:

Yes

1 Put the water into a bowl and sprinkle the gelatine over it. Leave to stand for a minute or two, then set on the back of the Aga until it has dissolved.
2 Put the rice, sugar, cardamom and milk into a pan and bring to the boil.
3 Cover the pan and transfer to the simmering oven for about an hour, until the rice has absorbed all of the milk.
4 Remove from the oven and allow the rice to cool completely.
5 Separate the egg and beat the yolk into the rice. Stir the gelatine into the rice. Whisk the egg white, then the cream and fold them into the rice.
6 Chill the pudding for an hour until set, then serve with fruit salad.

chocolate fudge pudding

To feed more people: Double all of the ingredients will feed up to 10 and will fill the large roasting tin

Serves 4

2 oz (55g) self raising flour
1 oz (25g) cocoa powder
3 oz (85g) softened butter
3 oz (85g) caster sugar
1 egg
2 oz (55g) sultanas
1 oz (25g) dark brown sugar

Sauce:

½ pint (275ml) hot black coffee
1 oz (25g) caster sugar
3 tbsp rum
Icing sugar to decorate

Oven:

Baking oven, 170C, 350F, Gas 4

Prepare ahead:

Will keep warm beside the Aga for up to an hour

Freeze:

No

1. Grease a 2 pint/l litre soufflé dish. Mix together flour, cocoa, butter, caster sugar and egg. Beat well and turn into soufflé dish. Sprinkle over the brown sugar and sultanas.
2. Mix the coffee, caster sugar and rum together and pour over the pudding.
3. 3 and 4 oven Aga: Set the dish on the grid shelf on the floor of the baking oven and bake for about 45 minutes.
4. 2 oven Aga: Set the dish into the large roasting tin and hang the tin onto the 4th runners in the roasting oven. Slide the cold plain shelf onto the 2nd runners above and bake for about 35 minutes.
5. Remove from the oven, dust with icing sugar and serve with cream.

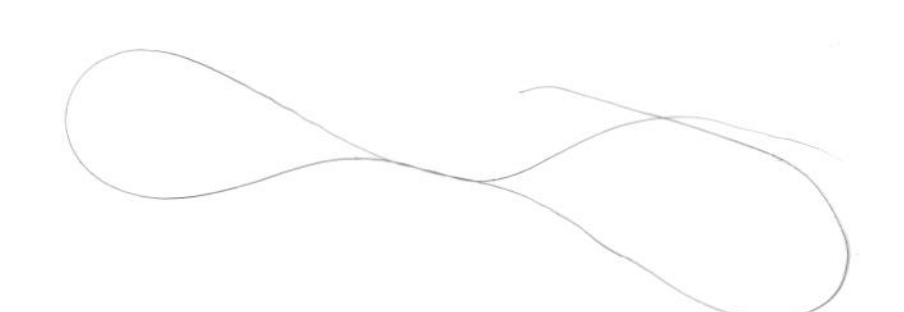

caramel and cholesterol pie

Serves 4

½ packet (125g) digestive biscuits
1 tbsp cocoa powder
2 oz (55g) butter

9 oz (250g) granulated sugar
6 tbsp water
Small pot (125ml) cream
4 oz (110g) butter
½ tsp Maldon salt

4 oz (110g) plain chocolate
2 oz (55g) butter
2 eggs
2 oz (55g) soft brown sugar

Oven:

Baking oven, 170C, 350F, Gas 4

Prepare in advance:

Will keep in the fridge for up to 24 hours

Freeze:

Yes

1. Put the 2 oz (55g) butter in a bowl on the back of the Aga to melt. Put the chocolate and 2 oz (55g) butter into another bowl on the back of the Aga to melt.
2. Crush the biscuits with the cocoa powder, then stir in the melted butter.
3. Line a 9"/23cm springform tin with Bake-O-Glide, and tip the biscuit mix into it. Spread it out and press down all over the base and up the sides of the tin. Refrigerate until needed.
4. Put the granulated sugar and water into a heavy based pan and set it onto the simmering plate. Swirl it about until the sugar has dissolved in the water, then boil it for about 5 minutes, until it darkens into a caramel.
5. Remove the pan from the heat and add the cream, salt and 4oz (110g) butter. It will spit, but be brave! Stir until it turns to a creamy gloop. Allow to cool.
6. Whisk the eggs and brown sugar together until foamy and light, then fold in the melted butter and chocolate.
7. Tip the caramel into the biscuit case, and spread the chocolate mixture over the top. Bake for about 15 minutes until beginning to brown.
8. 3 and 4 oven Aga: Hang the grid shelf on the 4th, lowest, runners in the baking oven and put the tin onto it.
9. 2 oven Aga: Put the tin into the large roasting tin and hang it from the 4th, lowest runners in the roasting oven. Slide the plain shelf onto the 2nd runners above.
10. Serve tepid, dusted with icing sugar.

grand marnier cheesecake

To feed more people: Double all of the ingredients will fill a 10"/25cm tin and will serve up to 15

Serves 6–8

Base:

8 oz (225g) digestive biscuits

4 oz (110g) butter

Filling:

6 tbsp caster sugar

2 egg yolks

5 fl oz (150ml) sour cream

2 oz (55g) plain chocolate

1 lb (450g) cream cheese

½ tsp vanilla extract

Juice of 1 lemon

3 tbsp Grand Marnier

Grated chocolate to decorate

Oven:

Simmering oven, 130C, 250F, Gas 1

Prepare ahead:

Cooked, cooled cheesecake will keep in the fridge for up to 24 hours

Freeze:

Yes

1. Set the butter in a bowl on the back of the Aga to melt. Put the packs of cream cheese on the back of the Aga to warm up and soften. Put the chocolate into a large bowl and set it on the back of the Aga to melt.
2. Slide the grid shelf onto the 3rd runners in the simmering oven.
3. Crush biscuits in a plastic bag with a rolling pin (or in food processor). Add the melted butter and stir well. Grease and line a loose based 8"/20cm flan tin and press in the biscuit mixture to make a base for the cheesecake. Chill or freeze until needed.
4. Whizz the cream cheese and half of the sour cream, the lemon juice, 4 tbsp sugar and egg yolks.
5. Tip half of the mixture into the bowl of melted chocolate and stir well. Pour this over the biscuit base.
6. Mix 2 tbsp of the Grand Marnier and the vanilla into the remaining half of the mixture and pour over the chocolate layer.
7. Mix together the remaining sour cream, 1 tbsp liqueur and 2 tbsp sugar and pour over the cheesecake.
8. Carefully, so as not to disturb the layers, put into the simmering oven and bake for 30 minutes, until set.
9. Cool, chill for a couple of hours then remove from the tin – put the cheesecake onto a plate and serve decorated with grated chocolate.

pecan and ginger tart

To feed more people: Double the ingredients will fill a 12"/30cm flan case and will feed up to 14

Serves 6

Pastry:

6 oz (175g) plain flour
3 oz (75g) butter
1 oz (25g) caster sugar
1 egg yolk
2 tbsp cold water
½ tsp ground ginger

Filling:

5 oz (150g) pecan nuts
3 balls stem ginger
1 tub (150g) mascarpone
3 eggs
2 oz (55g) dark brown sugar

Oven:

Roasting oven, 200C, 400F, Gas 6

Prepare in advance:

Cooked, cooled tart will keep in the fridge for up to 24 hours

Prepare ahead:

Will keep warm in the simmering or warming oven for up to an hour

Freeze:

Yes

1. To make the pastry, put the flour, sugar, butter, ginger and egg yolk into a processor and whizz to the consistency of breadcrumbs. With the motor running, add the water a little at a time, until it forms a dough. Roll out and line a 9"/23cm ceramic flan dish. Refrigerate until needed.
2. Put the tub of mascarpone onto the back of the Aga to soften.
3. Tip the pecan nuts into the pastry case.
4. Grate the stem ginger into a bowl, then add the eggs, mascarpone and sugar. Mix well, then pour over the pecan base, scatter on the flaked almonds and set onto the floor of the roasting oven.
5. Bake for about 25 minutes, until the pastry is brown and the top risen a little and golden.
6. Dust with icing sugar and serve tepid with crème fraîche.

lemon and lime meringue pie

To feed more people: Double the ingredients will fill a 12"/30cm flan dish and will serve up to 14

Serves 6

Base:

8 oz (225g) ginger nut biscuits

2 oz (55g) butter

1 oz (25g) light muscovado sugar

Filling:

2 limes

1 lemon

1 tin (400g) condensed milk

2 eggs

4 oz caster sugar

Oven:

Baking oven, 170C, 350F, Gas 4

Prepare in advance:

Will keep in the fridge for up to 24 hours

Freeze:

Yes

1. Put the butter in a bowl on the back of the Aga to melt, or melt it in a pan on the simmering plate.
2. Crush the biscuits and add them, with the sugar, to the melted butter.
3. Line a 9"/23cm loose based tin with Bake-O-Glide.
4. Tip the biscuit mix into the tin and press across the base and up the sides of the tin, then chill until set.
5. Grate the rind from the limes and lemon and squeeze the juice. Mix the juice and rind with the condensed milk, which will thicken.
6. Separate the eggs and stir the yolks into the lime mixture. Pour this into the prepared biscuit base.
7. Whisk the egg whites until thick, then whisk in all but 1 tbsp of the caster sugar, a spoonful at a time, until it is thick and shiny. Spoon this meringue over the top of the pie and make a swirly pattern on the top. Sprinkle with the remaining caster sugar.
8. 2 oven Aga: Set the pie into the large roasting tin and hang this from the 4th, lowest runners in the roasting oven. Slide the cold plain shelf onto the 2nd runners above and bake for about 10 minutes until the top is pale brown.
9. 3 and 4 oven Aga: Set the grid shelf on the floor of the baking oven and put the pie onto it. Bake for 15 minutes until the top is pale brown.

muscovado cheesecake

To feed more people: Double the ingredients will fill an 11"/28cm tin and will feed up to 10

Serves 4–5

Base:

2 oz (55g) butter

5 oz (150g) ginger nut biscuits

Filling:

3 tsp gelatine powder (one sachet)

2 tbsp boiling water

14 oz (400g tub) crème fraîche

6 oz dark muscovado sugar

1 tsp vanilla extract

14 oz (2 x 200g tubs) cream cheese

Oven:

Back of Aga

Prepare in advance:

Will keep in the fridge for 24 hours

Prepare ahead:

Will keep in the fridge for 24 hours

Freeze:

Yes

1. Set the butter in a bowl on the back of the Aga to melt. Set the cream cheese onto the back of the Aga to soften.
2. Crush the biscuits and stir them into the butter.
3. Line an 8"/20cm loose based tin with Bake-O-Glide and spread the biscuit mixture over it. Press down all over the base of the tin, then chill or freeze until needed.
4. Pour the boiling water into a small bowl and sprinkle the gelatine over it. Leave for a minute, then stir until dissolved.
5. Mix together the crème fraîche and muscovado sugar, then stir in the vanilla extract and dissolved gelatine. Beat in the cream cheese, then pour this onto the biscuit base. Cover and chill for at least a couple of hours until set. Remove the tin and put the cheesecake onto a plate.
6. Serve at room temperature, with a dusting of icing sugar to show you have made an effort.

sweet grape pudding

To feed more people: Double the ingredients will feed up to 10 in individual bowls or glasses

Serves 4

1 lb (450g) seedless grapes

2 tbsp light muscovado sugar

1 pint (500ml tub) thick yogurt

Oven:

Simmering oven, 130C, 250F, Gas 1

Prepare in advance:

Cooked, cooled pudding will keep in the fridge for up to 24 hours, but serve at room temperature

Freeze:

No, the grapes go soggy

1. Remove the grapes from their stalks.
2. Line a large shallow baking tray with Bake-O-Glide.
3. Pile the grapes into the tin and shake to distribute evenly.
4. Sprinkle with the sugar.
5. Bake in the simmering oven for about three hours, until the grapes are sticky and tender.
6. Tip into a bowl with the yogurt, stir to mix and serve.

Aga tip: Pretty much any fruit can be cooked in the simmering oven like this, to concentrate its sweetness for a really simple, healthy pudding

white chocolate and raspberry cheesecake

To feed more people: Make two cheesecakes to cut into 16 slices

Serves 6–8

9 oz (250g) white chocolate
2 tubs (2 x 300g) cream cheese
½ pint (300ml) whipping cream
2 oz (55g) caster sugar
½ jar best quality raspberry jam
3½ oz (100g) ginger nut biscuits
8 oz (225g) raspberries
Icing sugar to finish

Oven:

Back of Aga

Prepare in advance:

Prepared cheesecake will keep in fridge for 24 hours

Freeze:

Yes

1. Put the chocolate into a bowl and set on the back of the Aga to melt. Set the packets of cream cheese onto the back of the Aga to soften.
2. Put the biscuits into a plastic bag and bash with a rolling pin to break them up, but not to a powder.
3. Line a 2lb/1litre loaf tin with cling film.
4. Put the cream cheese, cream and sugar into a bowl and whisk together until thick.
5. Mix half of the raspberries with the jam.
6. Put half of the cheese mixture into the tin and smooth the top. Spread with the mixed raspberries and jam.
7. Spread the rest of the cream cheese over the top, then put on the biscuits in a single layer. Press down gently, cover with more cling film and chill for at least 4 hours or overnight.
8. To serve, turn the cheesecake out of the tin, remove the cling film and scatter over the rest of the raspberries and shake a little icing sugar over the top to show you have made an effort!

Alternatives:
- Use broken meringues instead of the ginger biscuits
- Use strawberry jam and sliced strawberries instead of the raspberries
- Use marmalade and orange segments and dark chocolate for a winter version
- Use cranberry sauce and poached cranberries with orange juice for a Christmas version
- Make individual cheesecakes by using a 12 hole deep muffin tin, lining each hole with cling film

blackberry and apple frangipane tart

To feed more people: Double the ingredients will fill a 12"/30cm flan tin and will cut into 12 pieces

Serves 6

Pastry:

6 oz (175g) plain flour
3 oz (75g) butter
1 oz (25g) caster sugar
1 egg yolk
2 tbsp cold water
½ tsp almond extract

Filling:

2 cooking apples
4 oz (110g) blackberries
2 eggs
1 tub (150g) mascarpone
2 oz (55g) ground almonds
3 oz (75g) caster sugar
2 oz (55g) flaked almonds

Oven:

Roasting oven, 400F, 200C, Gas 6

Prepare in advance:

Cooked, cooled tart will keep in the fridge for up to 24 hours

Prepare ahead:

Will keep warm in the simmering or warming oven for half an hour, or will cool gently beside the Aga for an hour or so

Freeze:

Yes, either as the finished tart, or just freeze the pastry case in its dish, in which case you can pile in the filling and cook the pastry from frozen

1. To make the pastry, put the flour, sugar, butter, almond extract and egg yolk into a processor and whizz to the consistency of breadcrumbs. With the motor running, add the water a little at a time, until it forms a dough. Roll out and line a 9"/23cm ceramic flan dish. Refrigerate until needed.
2. Put the tub of mascarpone onto the back of the Aga to soften.
3. To assemble the tart, peel core and quarter the apples, chop into small pieces and scatter them over the pastry case. Spread the blackberries on top of the apples.
4. Mix together the eggs, mascarpone, sugar and almonds. Whisk the whites and fold in to the mixture, then pour over the apple and blackberry base, scatter on the flaked almonds and set onto the floor of the roasting oven. Bake for about 25 minutes, until the pastry is brown and the top risen a little and golden.
5. Dust with icing sugar and serve tepid with crème fraîche.

apple and cranberry pudding

To feed more people: Double all of the ingredients will fill a 4 pint/2 litre bowl and will serve up to 10

Serves 4

4 oz (110g) butter

6 oz (175g) wholemeal self raising flour

½ tsp baking powder

4 oz (110g) light muscovado sugar

2 eggs

2 tbsp milk

2 large Bramley apples

1 pack (170g) dried cranberries

Oven:

Simmering oven, 130C, 250F, Gas 1

Prepare in advance:

Will keep in fridge for up to 24 hours after cooking

Prepare ahead:

Keep warm for up to 2 hours in simmering oven

Freeze:

Yes

1. Set the butter in a bowl and put beside the Aga to soften.
2. Peel and roughly chop the apples.
3. Line a 2 pint/1 litre pudding basin with cling film.
4. Tip the flour, baking powder, sugar, eggs, and milk into the bowl of softened butter and beat well. Add the chopped apples and cranberries and mix in. Pour this into the pudding basin.
5. Make a lid for the basin with cling film.
6. Take a large pan and fill with about 1 inch / 2.5cm water. Lower in the pudding basin. Cover.
7. Bring to the boil then transfer to the simmering oven for at least 2½ hours.
8. Serve with custard or cream. Or both.

christmas ice cream

To feed more people: Share it? This is a one person one bowl pudding – some of us can eat the whole thing in one go . . .

Serves 4

1 tin condensed milk
1 pint (550ml) double cream
12 oz (375g) mixed dried fruit – a Christmassy selection of sultanas, raisins, glacé cherries, mixed peel, etc.
3 tbsp rum
1 tsp mixed spice

Oven:
Simmering oven, 130C, 250F, Gas 1

Prepare in advance:
Keep in freezer for a couple of weeks. Or longer

Freeze:
Of course!

1. Put the unopened tin of condensed milk into a pan and cover with cold water. Set the pan onto the boiling plate and bring to the boil. Cover the pan and transfer to the simmering oven for about three hours. Remove from the oven and leave to cool completely. *Alternatively, buy a tin of Carnation Caramel, which is exactly the same, but cooked in a factory not an Aga!*
2. Put the dried fruit into a bowl and add the rum. Cover and leave to absorb the rum while the caramel is in the oven.
3. Open the tin of condensed caramelised milk. Do not eat all of it immediately, as you need it for the ice cream.
4. Whip the cream until it is just starting to thicken, then stir in the condensed caramel.
5. Stir in the soaked fruit and the mixed spice – and maybe a grating of nutmeg if you have some to hand?
6. Pile the mixture into a 2 pint/1 litre pudding basin, cover and freeze until needed.
7. At least an hour before serving, remove from the freezer to soften. Turn out onto a plate so it looks like a Christmas pudding and serve in slices. Maybe with some hot traditional Christmas pudding?

pear and ginger pudding

To feed more people: Double the ingredients will fill a 4 pint/2 litre pudding basin and might feed as many as 12

Serves 4

2 pears, peeled and sliced

2 tbsp stem ginger, grated

2 tbsp ginger syrup from jar

2 large eggs

6 oz (175g) self raising flour

4 oz (110g) caster sugar

4 oz (110g) butter (softened beside the Aga for half an hour)

Sauce:

½ pint (275ml) double cream

4 oz (110g) butter

6 oz (170g) dark brown sugar

Oven:

Simmering oven, 130C, 250F, Gas 1

Prepare in advance:

Pudding is nicest eaten on the day it is made. Sauce will keep in the fridge for 48 hours

Prepare ahead:

Will keep warm in the simmering oven for an extra hour or so

Freeze:

No

1. Line a 2 pint/1 litre pudding basin with cling film.
2. Melt the butter for sauce and cook pears in the butter for 3 minutes.
3. Remove from heat and spoon the pears into the prepared bowl.
4. Add the brown sugar and cream to the pan. Bring to the boil and simmer for 5 minutes. Pour about a third of the sauce onto the pears.
5. Beat together the softened butter, caster sugar, flour, eggs, ginger and syrup. Pour into the bowl on top of pears.
6. Cover with cling film, then put the bowl into a deep pan with an inch of water in it. Bring to the boil then cover and transfer to the simmering oven for about 2½ hours.
7. Turn out and serve with the remaining sauce, warmed, and crème fraîche.

The sauce is also nice with sliced bananas, or sliced ripe pears, or with a teaspoon straight from the fridge . . .

new york cheeecake for sam

To feed more people: Double the ingredients will fill a 12"/30cm tin and will serve up to 16

Serves 6–8

4 oz (100g) digestive biscuits
2 oz (55g) butter
1½ lb (3 x 200g packs) cream cheese
4 oz (110g) soft light brown sugar
4 eggs
¼ pint (150ml) milk
½ pint (300ml) soured cream or crème fraîche
2 tsp vanilla extract
1 oz (25g) plain flour

Oven:

Baking oven, 175C, 350F, Gas 4

Prepare in advance:

Cooked, cooled cheesecake will keep in the fridge for 24 hours

Freeze:

Yes

1. Set the packet of cream cheese onto the back of the Aga to soften. Put the butter in a pan onto the simmering plate to melt.
2. Crush the biscuits and stir them into the pan of melted butter.
3. Line a 9"/23cm springform tin with Bake-O-Glide.
4. Pour the biscuit mixture into the tin and press down firmly.
5. Beat together the cream cheese, sugar, eggs, milk, soured cream, vanilla and flour until smooth, then pour into the prepared tin.
6. 3 and 4 oven Aga: Set the tin onto the grid shelf on the floor of the baking oven and bake for about an hour until golden brown.
7. 2 oven Aga: Set the tin into the large roasting tin and hang this on the 4th, lowest, runners in the roasting oven. Slide the plain shelf onto the 2nd runners above. After about 30 minutes, transfer the roasting tin, and its contents, to the simmering oven for a further 45 minutes.
8. Take the cake from the oven while it is still slightly wobbly in the centre and allow to cool.
9. When cold, chill for at least 2 hours, then serve in slices with some fruit.

rhubarb and ginger pudding

To feed more people: Double the ingredients will fill a 4 pint/2 litre pudding basin and might feed up to 12

Serves 4–6

3 balls stem ginger from a jar, plus
2 tbsp of the syrup
1 lb (450g) rhubarb
4 oz (110g) light muscovado sugar
4 oz (110g) butter
2 eggs
1 tsp vanilla extract
5 oz (150g) self raising flour

Oven:

Roasting oven 200C, 400F, Gas 6, and simmering oven, 130C, 250F, Gas 1

Prepare in advance:

Roast the rhubarb in advance but the pudding is nicest eaten on the day it is made

Prepare ahead:

Leave in simmering or warming oven for another hour if necessary

Freeze:

Roasted rhubarb, but not the whole pudding.

1. Trim the rhubarb and cut into 1"/2.5cm lengths.
2. Grate the stem ginger. Set the butter in a bowl beside the Aga to soften.
3. Line a small roasting tin with Bake-O-Glide and tip the rhubarb into it, with the ginger syrup.
4. Hang the tin from the 4th runners in the roasting oven for about 10 minutes, until the rhubarb is softened and bubbling.
5. Line a 2 pint/1 litre pudding basin with cling film. Put about half of the rhubarb into the bowl.
6. Beat together the butter, sugar, eggs, flour and vanilla. Stir in the grated ginger and the remaining rhubarb.
7. Tip this mixture into the prepared bowl and cover with cling film.
8. Put about an inch/2.5cm of water into a large pan, put in the bowl and put on the lid. Bring to the boil on the boiling plate, then transfer the whole thing to the simmering oven for at least 2 hours, up to 4 hours if necessary.
9. To serve, remove from the pan, take off the cling film lid and upend onto a plate. The rhubarb in the bottom of the bowl will cascade down the sides of the pudding.
10. Serve with custard (and cream!).

Aga tip: Roast gooseberries instead of rhubarb in season, or plums in the autumn for a really intense flavour

pear and ginger tart

To feed more people: Double the ingredients will fill a 12"/30cm flan dish and will cut into 12 slices

Serves 6

Pastry:

- 6 oz (175g) plain flour
- 3 oz (75g) butter
- 1 oz (25g) caster sugar
- 1 egg yolk
- 2 tbsp cold water
- ½ tsp ground ginger

Filling:

- 2 ripe pears
- 2 balls preserved stem ginger
- 1 tub (150g) mascarpone
- 2 eggs
- 3 oz (75g) caster sugar
- 1 oz (25g) flaked almonds

Oven:

Roasting oven, 200C, 400F, Gas 6

Prepare in advance:

Tart will keep in the fridge for up to 24 hours

Prepare ahead:

Will keep warm in the simmering or warming oven for up to an hour

Freeze:

Yes, but as it is nicest eaten on the day the pastry is cooked; freeze the pastry case alone, then fill and cook it from frozen for an almost instant pudding

1. To make the pastry, put the flour, sugar, butter, ginger and egg yolk into a processor and whizz to the consistency of breadcrumbs. With the motor running, add the water a little at a time, until it forms a dough. Roll out and line a 9"/23cm ceramic flan dish. Refrigerate until needed.
2. Put the tub of mascarpone onto the back of the Aga to soften.
3. To assemble the tart, peel, core and quarter the pears and slice them into the pastry case.
4. Grate the stem ginger into a bowl, then add the eggs, mascarpone and sugar. Mix well, then pour over the pear base, scatter on the flaked almonds and set onto the floor of the roasting oven. Bake for about 25 minutes, until the pastry is brown and the top risen a little and golden.
5. Dust with icing sugar and serve tepid with crème fraîche.

Aga tip: Try using roasted gooseberries or roasted rhubarb in the tart instead of the pears

pumpkin and pecan pie

To feed more people: Double the ingredients will fill a 12"/30cm flan dish and will cut into 12 pieces

Serves 4–6

Pastry:

6 oz plain flour

3 oz butter

½ tsp ground cinnamon

2–3 tbsp water

Filling:

4 oz (110g) pecan nuts

1 small pumpkin or butternut squash

1 tub (200g) mascarpone

3 eggs

1 tsp ground cinnamon

2 tbsp maple syrup

2 oz (55g) dark brown sugar

Oven:

Roasting oven, 200C, 400F, Gas 6

Prepare in advance:

Cooked, cooled pie will keep in the fridge for up to 24 hours

Prepare ahead:

Will keep warm in the simmering or warming oven for an hour, or cool slowly beside the Aga

Freeze:

Yes, either the complete, cooked pie or just the raw pastry in its dish, ready to tip in the filling and bake from frozen

1. Put the pumpkin or squash into the roasting oven and roast for 45 minutes. Remove from the oven and leave to cool.
2. Set the tub of mascarpone onto the back of the Aga to soften.
3. To make the pastry, put the flour, butter and cinnamon into a processor and whizz until the texture of breadcrumbs. With the motor running, add the water a teaspoon at a time until it comes together as a dough.
4. Roll out the pastry and line a 9"/23cm flan dish. Chill (or freeze) until required.
5. For the filling, halve the pumpkin or squash and peel away the skin and pips. You need about 12 oz (675g) of cooked pumpkin.
6. Put the pumpkin into a processor, with the eggs, softened mascarpone, maple syrup, sugar and spice. Whizz to a gloop.
7. Pour into the pastry case, scatter over the nuts and put onto the floor of the roasting oven for 25 minutes until set and golden.

Aga tip: Add flavours to pastry such as spices, herbs, lemon zest, cocoa, wholemeal flour, etc. to show that it is home made!

rice pudding

To feed more people: Double the ingredients will feed up to 9, but will need an extra half an hour in the simmering oven

Serves 4

1 oz (25g) butter
2 oz (55g) pudding rice
2 oz (55g) caster sugar
Few grates of nutmeg
1 pint (550ml) milk

Oven:

Simmering oven, 250F, 130C, Gas 2

Prepare in advance:

Cooled pudding will keep in the fridge for 24 hours, reheat in simmering oven for an hour or eat cold, standing in front of the fridge

Prepare ahead:

Will keep warm in the simmering oven for an extra hour or so

Freeze:

No

1. Put the butter into an oven proof dish and set on the back of the Aga to melt.
2. Put the rice, sugar, nutmeg and milk into a pan on the simmering plate and bring to the boil, stirring occasionally.
3. Simmer for 5 minutes, then pour into the hot buttery dish and set on the grid shelf on the floor of the roasting oven for 5 minutes, then transfer to the simmering oven for an hour, until all the milk has been absorbed.
4. (For a faster pudding, use flaked rice and cook for half an hour.)

Aga tip: Bringing the pudding to the boil before putting it into the simmering oven reduces the time it takes to cook quite dramatically. If you want a seriously slow pudding, put all the cold ingredients into a cold bowl and put into the simmering oven for 4 hours or longer

spotted dick

To feed more people: Double the ingredients will fill a 4 pint/2 litre bowl and will take an extra hour in the simmering oven

Serves 4

10 oz (300g) self raising flour

1 tsp baking powder

5 oz (150g) shredded suet

3 oz (85g) caster sugar

6 oz (175g) mixed currants and raisins

1 lemon

7 fl oz (200ml) milk

Oven:

Simmering oven, 130C, 250F, Gas 1

Prepare in advance:

Uncooked pudding will keep in the fridge for 6 hours

Prepare ahead:

Leave the pudding in the simmering or move to the warming oven for an extra couple of hours

Freeze:

No, it sets like rock!

1. Put the flour, baking powder, shredded suet, caster sugar, currants and grated rind of the lemon into a bowl and mix together.
2. Add the milk and stir to make a soft dough.
3. Line a 2 pint/1 litre pudding basin with cling film and tip the mixture into the basin. Cover with more cling film.
4. Take the Aga cake baker and fill to about 1½" depth with cold water; and add a slice of the lemon.
5. Put the bowl into the trivet and lower it into the pan. Put on the lid. Set the pan onto the boiling plate and bring to the boil.
6. Transfer the pan to the simmering oven and cook for about 2–4 hours.
7. Serve the spotted dick with lots of custard or cream, or both.

Aga tip: Steamed puddings are the nuclear weapons in the battle of the sexes, so make sure you know what it is you are after before you cook this – it is in the simmering oven long enough for a trip to the travel agents …

chocolate hazelnut dream

Looks like a lot of work, but it is really worth the effort

Serves up to 10 – possibly!

Cake:

4 oz (110g) plain chocolate
1 oz (25g) salted butter
3 oz (85g) soft brown sugar
3 egg whites
1 oz (25g) cocoa powder
4 oz (110g) chopped hazelnuts
2 tbsp strong black coffee

Middle layer:

4 oz (110g) white chocolate
7 oz tub (200g) mascarpone

Topping:

4 oz (110g) plain chocolate
¼ pint (150ml) double cream

Wrapping:

4 oz (110g) white chocolate

To finish:

Small bag Maltesers

Oven:

Baking oven, 170C, 350F, Gas 4

Prepare in advance:

Keeps in the fridge for up to 24 hours

Freeze:

Yes

1 Put the four amounts of chocolate into separate bowls. Add the butter to one of the bowls of dark chocolate and set all four on the back of the Aga to melt.
2 Set the tub of mascarpone onto the back of the Aga to soften.
3 Line a 9"/23cm round springform tin with Bake-O-Glide.
4 Whisk the egg whites until firm, then whisk in the sugar, a little at a time. Add the melted plain chocolate, cocoa, hazelnuts and coffee and fold together. Pour into the prepared tin.
5 2 oven Aga: Set the tin into the large roasting tin and hang it from the 4th runners in the roasting oven. Slide the cold plain shelf onto the 2nd runners above.
6 3 and 4 oven Aga: Set the grid shelf on the floor of the baking oven and put the tin onto it.
7 Bake the cake for about 20 minutes until risen and set. Remove from the oven and allow to cool in the tin.
8 Mix the soft mascarpone with a bowl of melted white chocolate and pour this over the cooled cake in the tin. Smooth the top and chill until set.
9 Whip the cream and stir in the second bowlful of melted plain chocolate. Pour this over the cake, smooth the top and once again, chill until set.
10 Take a piece of Bake-O-Glide or silicone paper long enough to wrap around the outside of the cake. Loosen the springform tin and slide the cake onto a plate.
11 This bit is optional but very effective: Spread the final bowlful of melted white chocolate onto the paper and wrap this around the cake. Chill for at least an hour until set, then remove the paper, tip the maltesers onto the top and serve the cake with some fruit to offset all that cream!

treacle and walnut tart

To feed more people: Double the ingredients will fill at 12"/30cm flan dish and should cut into 12 portions

Serves 4–6

Pastry:

6 oz plain flour

3 oz butter

Grated rind of a lemon

2–3 tbsp water

Filling:

3 slices bread

2 oz (55g) walnut halves

5 tbsp golden syrup

Juice of a lemon

Oven:

Roasting oven, 200C, 400F, Gas 6

Prepare in advance:

Cooked, cooled tart will keep in the fridge for up to 24 hours

Prepare ahead:

Will keep warm in the simmering or warming oven for up to an hour

Freeze:

Yes

1. To make the pastry, put the flour, butter and lemon rind into a processor and whizz until the texture of breadcrumbs. With the motor running, add the water a teaspoon at a time until it comes together as a dough.
2. Roll out the pastry and line a 9"/23cm flan dish. Chill (or freeze) until required.
3. For the filling, grate or process the bread to crumbs. Mix with the syrup, walnuts and lemon juice.
4. Pour into the pastry case and put onto the floor of the roasting oven for 25 minutes until set and golden.

lavender custard tart

Serves 4–6

6 oz (175g) plain flour
1 oz (25g) caster sugar
3 oz (75g) butter
2 tbsp cold water

Filling:

7 oz (200g) tub natural yogurt
¼ pint (150ml) creamy milk
4 oz (110g) caster sugar
3 eggs
6 lavender heads

Oven:

Roasting oven

Prepare in advance:

Refrigerate the cooked, cooled tart for 24 hours

Prepare ahead:

Tart will keep for up to an hour beside the Aga, gently cooling

Freeze:

Yes, make the pastry and freeze it, uncooked, until needed. Complete tart is nicest eaten on the day it is baked

1. Put the milk and yogurt into a bowl with the sugar and set on the back of the Aga to warm. Crush the lavender heads and stir into the milk mixture.
2. To make the pastry, whizz the flour, caster sugar and butter in a processor. Add sufficient water to bind into dough. Roll out and line a 9"/23cm flan dish. Chill for at least half an hour.
3. Beat the eggs and add to the yogurt and milk mixture. Pour into the pastry case.
4. Bake on the floor of the roasting oven for 25 minutes. Serve warm.

baked banana pudding

To feed more people: Double the ingredients will fill the large roasting tin and should give up to 10 portions

Serves 4–6

4 large bananas
4 oz (110g) sultanas
6 tbsp maple syrup
3 oz (85g) butter
4 oz (110g) soft brown sugar
2 eggs
6 oz (175g) wholemeal self raising flour
1 bag (100g) pecan nuts

Oven:

Baking oven, 170C, 350F, Gas 3

Prepare in advance:

Mix the pudding together and chill for up to 6 hours before baking

Prepare ahead:

Will keep warm in simmering or warming oven for up to an hour, or serve tepid

Freeze:

Don't see why not!

1. Set the butter in a bowl beside the Aga to soften for up to 30 minutes.
2. Peel the bananas and slice them into ¼"/1cm pieces.
3. Line the small roasting tin with Bake-O-Glide, or use a ceramic ovenproof dish of about the same size and shape.
4. Arrange about half of the banana slices over the base of the dish or tin. Pour over the maple syrup.
5. Mix together the softened butter, sugar, eggs and flour, then stir in the nuts.
6. Mash the remaining banana and add this to the sponge mixture, then spread it over the slices of banana in the dish.
7. 2 oven Aga: Set the dish or tin into the large roasting tin and hang this from the 4th, lowest, runners in the roasting oven. Slide the cold plain shelf onto the 2nd runners above.
8. 3 and 4 oven Aga: Hang the tin on the 4th, lowest, runners in the baking oven.
9. Bake the pudding for about 35 minutes until golden and puffed up but still very slightly wobbly. Leave in the tin to cool for about 5 minutes, then turn out onto a plate and serve.
10. If cooking in a ceramic serving dish, don't turn it out!
11. Serve with cream or crème fraîche or custard, or all three.

strawberry and orange bake

To feed more people: Double the ingredients will feed up to 12, but will need an extra 15 minutes in the oven

Serves 4–6

12 oz (340g) strawberries
1 tbsp orange juice
Grated rind of ½ an orange
5 oz (150g) caster sugar
2 eggs
4 oz (110g) butter
6 oz (175g) self-raising flour
1 tsp baking powder
Grated rind of half an orange
2 tbsp orange juice

Oven:

Baking oven, 170C, 375F, Gas 4

Prepare in advance:

Prepare the strawberries up to 24 hours in advance and chill, but the cake topping will rise better if made just before baking

Prepare ahead:

Will keep warm in simmering or warming oven for up to an hour

Freeze:

Yes

1. Grease a large ovenproof dish. Set the butter beside the Aga to soften.
2. Cut the strawberries into chunks and put into the base of the greased dish. Grate the orange rind over and pour on the juice. Shake to coat the berries in the juice.
3. Mix together 4 oz (110g) of the sugar, butter, eggs, flour, baking powder, orange juice and rind, then pour over the fruit. Sprinkle the remaining sugar on top.
4. 3 and 4 oven Aga: Set the grid shelf on the 4th runners in the baking oven and cook the pudding on this for about 25 minutes until risen and browned.
5. 2 oven Aga: Put the dish onto the grid shelf on the floor of the roasting oven and slide the cold plain shelf onto the second set of runners. Bake for about 25 minutes.
6. Serve dusted with icing sugar and some vanilla ice cream.

Aga tip: Baking the strawberries intensifies their sweetness, but the colour won't be a very bright red, as it fades in the oven

alix's beetroot brownies

Serves 24

- 1½ oz (40g) cocoa powder
- 4½ oz (120g) wholemeal plain flour
- 1½ tsp baking powder
- 5 oz (150g) light brown sugar
- 6 fl oz (175ml) apple purée (or apple sauce from a jar!)
- 4 tbsp strong black coffee
- 3 eggs
- 9 oz (250g) cooked beetroot
- 7 oz (200g) plain chocolate drops

Oven:

Baking oven, 180C, 350F, Gas 4

Prepare in advance:

Keeps well in a tin for two or three days

Prepare ahead:

Allow to cool slowly beside the Aga for an hour or so

Freeze:

Yes

1. Line the small roasting tin with Bake-O-Glide.
2. Grate the beetroot into a large bowl.
3. Add the cocoa, flour, baking powder, sugar and salt to the bowl and add the oil, vanilla extract, eggs and chocolate pieces and mix well.
4. Pour into the tin, and bake for approximately 50 minutes until risen and browned.
5. 2 oven Aga: Set the small roasting tin into the large roasting tin and hang from the 4th runners in the roasting oven, with the plain shelf on the 2nd runners above. After about 30 minutes, move the roasting tin and all its contents to the simmering oven for a further 25 minutes. Don't forget to take the plain shelf from the oven to cool down!
6. 3 and 4 oven Aga: Hang the small roasting tin from the 4th runners in the baking oven for about 50 minutes.
7. Serve warm with crème fraîche as a pudding, or cold for tea.

Aga tip: In a 2 oven Aga, baking cakes in the large roasting tin creates an 'oven within an oven' and prevents the heat from the sides of the oven causing crunchy edges to the cake

mincemeat muffins

An unusual alternative to mince pies – and about a third of the effort!

Makes 12

8 oz (225g) wholemeal self raising flour
4 oz (110g) caster sugar
1 tsp baking powder
1 egg
¼ pint (150ml) milk
¼ pint (150ml) sunflower oil
3 tbsp mincemeat

Oven:

Roasting oven, 190C, 375F, Gas 5

Prepare ahead:

Will keep in a tin for a day or so, but they are nicest eaten on the day they are baked!

Freeze:

Yes

1. Line a 12-hole muffin tin with paper or silicone cases.
2. Put the flour, sugar and baking powder into a bowl. Add the oil, milk and egg then stir to mix. Stir in the mincemeat, then pour into the muffin cases.
3. Set the grid shelf on the floor of the roasting oven and put the muffin tin on it.
4. You may need to slide the cold plain shelf onto the second set of runners after 15 minutes if the muffins are browning too quickly.
5. Bake for 20 minutes, until risen and golden.
6. Eat as soon as they are cool enough to handle, with a scattering of icing sugar on top to show you have made an effort!

Ring the changes:

- Add a spoonful of cocoa powder and some chocolate drops to the basic muffin mixture instead of the mincemeat
- Add 4 oz (110g) raspberries or blueberries to the basic mixture instead of the mincemeat
- Add a couple of spoons of jam or marmalade or lemon curd to the basic mixture instead of the mincemeat

courgette and hazelnut cake

Serves 8–10

- 6 oz (175g) butter
- 6 oz (175g) soft brown sugar
- 3 eggs
- 8 oz (225g) self raising flour
- 6 oz (175g) courgettes
- 1 medium cooking apple
- 4 oz (110g) chopped hazelnuts
- 4 oz (110g) whole hazelnuts

Oven:

Baking oven, 190C, 375F, Gas 5

Prepare in advance:

Keeps for a couple of days in an airtight tin

Freeze:

Yes

1. Set the butter in a bowl beside the Aga to soften.
2. Line the small roasting tin with Bake-O-Glide.
3. Trim, wash and grate the courgettes and apple.
4. Add the sugar, eggs and flour to the bowl of butter and mix together.
5. Add the courgettes, apple and chopped hazelnuts.

   Pile the mixture into the prepared tin, scatter over the whole hazelnuts and bake for about 25 minutes until golden.
6. 3 and 4 oven Aga: Hang the tin from the 3rd runners in the baking oven.
7. 2 oven Aga: Set the tin into the large roasting tin and hang that from the 4th runners in the roasting oven. Slide the plain shelf onto the 2nd runners above.
8. Leave the cooked cake in the tin to cool for 10 minutes, then turn out and cut into squares.

parsnip cake

Serves 4

8 oz (225g) butter

8 oz (225g) light muscovado sugar

4 eggs

1 lemon

10 oz (275g) wholemeal self raising flour

1 tsp baking powder

3 oz (100g bag) chopped hazelnuts

8 oz (225g) cooked parsnips

Topping:

7 oz (200g tub) cream cheese

5 oz (150g) icing sugar

Oven:

Baking oven, 180C, 350F, Gas 4

Prepare in advance:

Cake will keep in a tin for several days until someone finds it!

Freeze:

Yes

1. Set the butter in a bowl beside the Aga to soften. Set the cream cheese on the back of the Aga to soften.
2. Grate the rind of the lemon and squeeze the juice. Grate the parsnips.
3. Line an 8"/20cm square cake tin with Bake-O-Glide.
4. Beat together the softened butter, sugar, eggs, flour, baking powder, lemon rind and juice, then stir in the grated parsnips and chopped nuts.
5. Pile the mixture into the tin and bake for about an hour until risen and golden.
6. 2 oven Aga: Set the tin into the large roasting tin and hang it from the 4th runners in the roasting oven. Slide the plain shelf onto the 2nd runners above. After about 30 minutes, transfer the roasting tin with the cake in it to the simmering oven to continue cooking. Don't forget to remove the plain shelf from the oven to cool down!
7. 3 and 4 oven Aga: Set the grid shelf onto the floor of the oven and put the cake tin onto it.
8. Let the cake cool for 10 minutes in the tin before turning out onto a rack to cool completely.
9. For the topping: Beat together the cream cheese and icing sugar until smooth.
10. Cut the cake in half, spread half of the icing over the base, put the other half back on and top with the rest of the icing. Make some squiggly patterns on top with a fork to show that you have made an effort!

If you hate parsnips, try using cooked beetroot instead, either way, no one will ever guess what you have put into this very moist cake

cornish saffron loaf

Serves 4

1 pack (500g) white bread mix
2 oz (55g) butter
2 oz (55g) caster sugar
1 egg
About ½ pint (300ml) milk
12 oz (350g) sultanas
1 lemon
About 5 saffron threads

Topping:

1 oz (25g) butter
About 3 saffron threads

Oven:

Aga roasting oven, 200C, 400F, Gas 6

Prepare in advance:

Dough will rise slowly in fridge overnight

Prepare ahead:

Keeps in an airtight tin for 24 hours

Freeze:

Yes, slice before freezing so you can have just one piece (or two, or three) at a time for tea

1. Put the milk and saffron in a mug on the back of the Aga to warm up a little.
2. Squeeze the juice from the lemon and add to the sultanas, with a tablespoon of warm water. Set on the back of the Aga to plump up.
3. Tip the bread mix, sugar and butter into a processor and whizz until mixed, or rub the butter in by hand. Mix together the egg and about half of the milk, and add to the flour mixture. Mix with a round bladed knife and add the rest of the milk until it is a soft dough – you may not need all of the milk.
4. Knead the dough by hand or in a processor until it is really pliable.
5. Drain the sultanas and knead them into the dough.
6. Line an 8" square cake tin with Bake-O-Glide and put the dough into it. Set beside the Aga for about an hour, until it has doubled in size.
7. For the topping: Put the butter and saffron in a bowl on the back of the Aga to melt.
8. Bake the tin on the floor of the roasting oven for about 20 minutes until golden brown.
9. As soon as the loaf comes out of the oven, pour the flavoured, melted butter over it. Eat as soon as it is cool enough to slice!

Aga tip: Bread rises beautifully beside the Aga. If you want to rise it on top of the Aga, set the tin onto a folded towel or a chef's pad on the closed simmering plate lid – if the tin is in direct contact with the lid it is too hot and may kill the yeast in the bread

christmas flapjacks

Makes up to 24

6 oz (175g) butter
8 oz (235g) porridge oats
6 oz (175g) soft brown sugar
3 oz (75g) plain flour
½ tsp bicarbonate of soda
½ tsp salt
1 jar mincemeat

Oven:

Baking oven, 170C, 350F, Gas 4

Prepare in advance:

Will keep in a tin for a week, if well hidden

Freeze:

Yes

1. Put the butter into a large pan and set on the back of the Aga to melt. Put the jar of mincemeat onto the back of the Aga to soften and warm up.
2. Mix the oats, sugar, flour, salt and bicarbonate of soda, into the melted butter.
3. Line the small roasting tin with Bake-O-Glide.
4. Put half of the mixture into the tin and spread evenly.
5. Spread the jar of mincemeat over, and top with the rest of mixture.
6. 2 oven Aga: Set the tin into the large roasting tin and hang from the 4th runners in the roasting oven, with the plain shelf on the 2nd runners above.
7. 3 and 4 oven Aga: Hang the tin from the 3rd runners in the baking oven.
8. Bake for 25 minutes until golden brown.

classic victoria sandwich

Serves 4

3 eggs
The weight of the eggs in:
Caster sugar
Self raising flour
Butter

Pinch of salt
¼ tsp vanilla extract

Raspberry jam to fill
Caster sugar to finish

Oven:

Baking oven, 170C, 350F, Gas 4

Prepare in advance:

Will keep in a tin for a day or so, if well hidden

Freeze:

Yes

1. Set a pack of butter beside the Aga to soften for half an hour. Set the jar of jam onto the back of the Aga to warm up and soften.
2. Weigh the eggs. Weigh the butter, flour and sugar to the same weight as the eggs.
3. Mix together the butter, sugar, flour, eggs, salt and vanilla and beat well (if the butter is really soft, it should be very easy).
4. Line 2 x 7"/18cm cake tins with Bake-O-Glide.
5. Divide the mixture between the tins, then bake for about 20 minutes until the tops are browned and the cake springs back to the touch.
6. 2 oven Aga: Set the cake tins into the large roasting tin and hang it from the 4th runners in the roasting oven. Slide the plain shelf onto the 2nd runners above.
7. 3 and 4 oven Aga: Set the grid shelf onto the 4th runners in the baking oven and put the cake tins onto it to bake.
8. When the cakes are cooked, leave them in the tins to cool down for a few minutes, then turn out onto a rack to cool. Remove plain shelf from oven.
9. Spread one cake with raspberry jam and sandwich them together, and finish with a scattering of caster sugar.

Ring the changes:

- Add grated orange or lemon rind to the cakes, then sandwich together with lemon or orange flavoured icing
- Add a tablespoon of cocoa powder to the cake mix, then sandwich together with chocolate fudge icing
- Add chocolate drops to the cake mixture
- Add dried fruit to the cake mixture
- Add a spoonful of black treacle to the cake mixture and sandwich together with vanilla cream cheese frosting

welsh cakes

To feed more people: Double the ingredients will make 28 cakes

Makes 12

8 oz (225g) plain flour
3 oz (85g) caster sugar
½ tsp ground mixed spice
½ tsp baking powder
¼ tsp salt
4 oz (110g) butter
2 oz (55g) currants or sultanas
1 egg
1 tbsp milk (possibly!)

Oven:

Simmering plate

Prepare in advance:

Cakes will keep in a tin for a few days, if well hidden in a cupboard, reheat for a few seconds on simmering plate before serving

Prepare ahead:

Eat as soon as you can once they are cooked and still warm!

Freeze:

Yes

1. Put the flour, sugar, spice, salt, currants and baking powder into a mixer and add the butter. Mix until it resembles breadcrumbs, then add the egg and mix to a dough. If it is very crumbly, add a little milk to soften the dough.
2. Roll out the dough on a floured board and cut out 3"/8cm rounds with a cutter and re-roll the leftovers to make more rounds.
3. Put a piece of Bake-O-Glide onto the simmering plate and put the cakes onto it – about 8 at a time is plenty. Shut the lid and cook for about 3 minutes, then flip the cakes over to brown the other side. When they are crisp and brown on both sides, they are done.
4. Cook the rest of the cakes in batches, then serve with butter and strawberry jam.

Aga tip: Using Bake-O-Glide on the simmering plate saves washing up a pan!

ginger nuts

Makes about 12

- 4 oz (110g) self raising flour
- 1 oz (25g) caster sugar
- 2 oz (55g) butter
- ½ tsp bicarbonate of soda
- 1 tbsp ground ginger
- 2 tbsp golden syrup

Oven:

Baking oven,
190C, 375F, Gas 5

Prepare ahead:

Keeps for up to 3 days in an airtight tin

Freeze:

Yes

1. Line the cold plain shelf with Bake-O-Glide.
2. Put all ingredients into a bowl and mix together.
3. Roll into small balls and place on the plain shelf.
4. 3 and 4 oven Aga: Slide the shelf onto the 3rd runners in the baking oven.
5. 2 oven Aga: Slide the shelf onto the 4th, lowest, runners in the roasting oven. Slide the large roasting tin onto the 2nd runners above to act as a cold plain shelf.
6. Bake for 12–15 minutes until golden brown. Remove from the oven.
7. Lift the Bake-O-Glide off the shelf to allow the biscuits to cool quickly and transfer them to a wire rack.

Aga tip: If you are baking biscuits, or anything else, on the cold plain shelf, use the large roasting tin as a plain shelf above it to reduce the temperature in the oven

chocolate macaroons

To feed more people: Double the ingredients will make up to 36 single macaroons

Makes about 16, to sandwich together making 8, or 4 servings

5 oz (150g) ground almonds

9 oz (250g) icing sugar

1 oz (25g) cocoa powder

4 egg whites

Filling:

Small pot (128ml) double cream

1 oz (25g) icing sugar

¼ tsp vanilla extract

Oven:

Baking oven, 180C, 375F, Gas 4

Prepare in advance:

Macaroons will keep in a tin for several days, do not fill until the day of eating

Freeze:

Yes

1. Mix together the ground almonds, icing sugar and cocoa.
2. Whisk the egg whites until firm, then, still whisking, add the sugar mixture a spoonful at a time.
3. Line the cold plain shelf with Bake-O-Glide and spoon blobs of mixture onto the shelf. Bang this on the work surface to encourage the macaroons to spread and burst any air bubbles. Leave to stand for at least 10 minutes while they spread.
4. 2 oven Aga: Slide the macaroons on the shelf onto the 4th, lowest, runners in the roasting oven. Slide your large roasting tin onto the second runners above, to act as a plain shelf and shield the macaroons from the heat of the oven.
5. 3 and 4 oven Aga: Slide the shelf onto the 4th, lowest, runners in the baking oven.
6. Bake for about 12–15 minutes until set and golden. Cool on the shelf for 5 minutes, then gently lift off the Bake-O-Glide onto a cooling rack.
7. For the filling, whip the cream and stir in the sugar and vanilla. Sandwich the macaroons together in pairs and chill until ready to eat.

fork biscuits

Makes about 16

Biscuits:

2 oz (55g) caster sugar
5 oz (150g) self-raising flour
4 oz (110g) butter (room temperature if possible)

Flavouring – either
Grated rind of an orange, or
Grated rind of a lemon, or
1 tbsp cocoa powder, or
Few drops vanilla essence

Oven:

Roasting oven, 190C, 375F, Gas 5

Prepare in advance:

Will keep in a tin for a couple of days

Freeze:

Yes

1. Line the cold plain shelf with Bake-O-Glide.
2. Put the biscuit ingredients and chosen flavouring into a food processor and whizz until well mixed.
3. Using your hands, take lumps of mixture about the size of a walnut and roll into balls. Place on the Bake-O-Glide and flatten with the back of a fork dipped in water.
4. Slide the shelf into the 4th, lowest, runners in the roasting oven and bake for 10–15 minutes, until golden brown.
5. Lift the cooked biscuits from the sheet with a fish slice; they are liable to break at this stage!
6. Leave to cool and crisp on a wire rack.

chocolate coated fork biscuits

Melt 4 oz (110g) plain chocolate drops and dip vanilla flavoured fork biscuits into melted chocolate until they are half coated

jersey granny's sticky bread

To feed more people: Make two loaves to give up to 30 slices. Cut these in half to make 60 small slices

Cuts into about 14 slices

8 oz (230g) self-raising flour

1 tsp baking powder

Pinch salt

6 oz (170g) caster sugar

4 oz (110g) mixed dried fruit

6 fl oz (175ml) milk

1 egg

2 tbsp black treacle

Oven:

Baking oven, 350F, 180C, Gas 4

Prepare ahead:

Keeps up to 4 days in an airtight tin

Freeze:

Yes

1 Put the tin of treacle onto the back of the Aga to warm up and soften.
2 Grease and line a 2lb/1 kg loaf tin.
3 Beat all the ingredients together and pour into the prepared tin.
4 3 and 4 oven Aga: Slide the grid shelf onto the floor of the baking oven and set the loaf tin onto it.
5 2 oven Aga: Set the tin into the large roasting tin and hang that from the 4th runners in the roasting oven. Slide the plain shelf onto the 2nd runners above.
6 Bake for 1 hour until a skewer inserted into the centre of the cake comes away clean. Cool in the tin.
7 Serve cut into slices and spread with butter.

Aga tip: Warming the black treacle on the back of the Aga makes it much easier to pour and measure

rasperry shortcake

To feed more people: Double the mixture and a whole jar of jam will fill the large roasting tin and cut into as many as 60 small pieces

Makes 24 pieces

12 oz (325g) plain flour
8 oz (225g) butter
4 oz (110g) caster sugar
Pinch salt
½ jar (200g) raspberry jam
Icing sugar to finish

Oven:

Baking oven, 160C, 350F, Gas 4

Prepare ahead:

Will keep in an airtight tin for up to 48 hours

Freeze:

Yes

1. Set the jar of jam onto the back of the Aga to warm up and soften.
2. Line the small roasting tin with Bake-O-Glide.
3. Put the flour, sugar, salt and butter into a processor and whiz until the consistency of sand. Tip half of this into the tin and press down firmly – use the bottom of a tumbler if you don't want to get your hands covered in mixture!
4. Spread the jam over the tin, then tip in the rest of the shortcake mix. Spread over and press down firmly.
5. 3 and 4 oven Aga: Hang the tin from the second set of runners in the baking oven.
6. 2 oven Aga: Put the small tin into the large roasting tin and hang it from the lowest runners in the roasting oven – and slide the cold plain shelf onto the second set of runners above.
7. Cook for about 25 minutes until pale golden. Allow to cool before turning out, cutting into squares and dusting with a little icing sugar.

Ring the changes:

- Use marmalade instead of the jam
- Use lemon curd instead of the jam
- Use mincemeat instead of the jam to make the simplest (and best) mince pies ever!

elderflower cordial

Perfect on a summer's day, or try adding a spoonful to cooked gooseberries

Makes about 3 pints

24 heads of elderflower

2 lemons

2½ pints (1½ litres) water

2 lbs (900g) sugar

2 oz (55g) citric acid

Oven:

Simmering plate

Prepare ahead:

Will keep for a couple of weeks in the fridge

Freeze:

Yes

1. Put the sugar and water into a large pan and bring to the boil, stirring until the sugar has dissolved. Allow to boil for 2 minutes, then remove from the heat and set aside to cool.
2. Pick the elderflowers and shake each head vigorously to dislodge any wildlife lurking within.
3. Scrub and halve the lemons and squeeze out the juice, then roughly chop the skins. Put the lemon juice, skins, citric acid and flowers into a large bowl and pour on the cooled sugar syrup. Stir well and cover tightly then leave in a cool place to macerate for at least 48 hours, stirring occasionally.
4. Strain the cordial into bottles and store in the fridge for 2 weeks or freeze. Serve diluted with water – either still or sparkling.

Ring the changes:

Use oranges or limes instead of lemon

Aga tip: buy citric acid from a home brew shop. It's much cheaper than a chemist

summer punch

Serves 4

- 1/3 cucumber
- 1 lime
- 8 oz (225g) green seedless grapes
- Handful mint leaves
- 2 pints (1 litre) white grape juice
- 2 pints (1 litre) fizzy water
- 2 tbsp rose water
- Ice cubes

Prepare in advance:

Prepare the fruit up to 24 hours in advance, pour on the grape juice but add the fizzy water and ice just before serving

1. Wash and slice the cucumber and lime. Remove the grapes from their stalks, then wash them. Tear up the mint leaves.
2. Put all the fruit and leaves into a large jug.
3. Put lots of ice cubes into the jug, then pour on the grape juice and fizzy (or should I say sparkling?) water. Add the rose water and stir.
4. Serve.

sloe gin

Makes 1 bottle

- 1 bottle of gin (70cl)
- 8 oz (225g) sloes
- 6 oz (175g) sugar

1. Put the sloes into a plastic bag and bash them a couple of times with a rolling pin (alternatively, prick each one ten times with a darning needle).
2. Pour the sloes, gin and sugar into a large bottle, put a lid on tightly and shake.
3. Shake the bottle once a day for a fortnight, then once a week for 3 months.
4. Drain the liquid into a clean bottle, discard the spent sloes and enjoy at once or allow to mature for another month.

old fashioned salad cream

Makes 3 x 12oz (340g) jars

8 oz (225g) icing sugar

12 fl oz (300ml) clear malt vinegar

3 eggs

1½ oz (35g) mustard powder

8 fl oz (200ml) sunflower oil

1 tsp salt

Prepare ahead:

Keeps for 2 weeks in fridge

Freeze:

No

1 Rinse three jam jars and put them, still wet, into the simmering oven.

2 Put the sugar and vinegar into a pan and warm until the sugar has dissolved.

3 Put the eggs, mustard and salt into a processor and, with the motor running, gradually pour in the oil and whizz until emulsified. Then, still whizzing, slowly add the sugar and vinegar mixture.

4 Pour into a large bowl and set over a pan of boiling water on the simmering plate. Cook the salad cream, stirring continuously, until thickened – this takes 5–10 minutes.

5 Pour into the hot, sterile jars, seal then cool and refrigerate.

michaelmas chutney

Makes about 10 jars

- 2 lb (900g) green tomatoes
- 2 lb (900g) bananas (yes, really!)
- 2 lb (900g) cooking apples
- 1 lb (450g) crystallised ginger
- 2 lb (900g) onions
- 3 lb (1.35kg) soft brown sugar
- 2 lb (900g) sultanas
- 3 tbsp sea salt
- 5 pints (3 litres) malt vinegar

Oven:

Simmering oven, 130C, 250F, Gas 1 and floor of roasting oven

Prepare in advance:

Chutney needs about a month to mature

Freeze:

No need

1. Wash 10 jam jars and put them, still wet, into the simmering oven.
2. Chop the tomatoes. Peel, core and grate the apples. Peel and grate the onions. Put all these into a preserving pan with the vinegar and bring to the boil, then cover and move to the simmering oven for 2 hours.
3. Peel and grate the bananas and ginger and add to the pan with the sultanas, sugar and salt.
4. Set the pan onto the boiling plate to bring it back to the boil, then cover again and return the pan to the simmering oven for a further hour.
5. When all the vegetables are soft, remove the pan lid and transfer to the floor of the roasting oven to boil and reduce until smooth and thick.
6. Pot and seal. Eat after 6 weeks.

Tip: Boiling the chutney on the floor of the oven to reduce it means that all the vinegar smells go up the chimney or flue, so that the kitchen does not smell of cooking vinegar for days after you have made your chutney!

the witch's pickle

Makes about 6 jars

A large handful of fresh red chillies
3 cooking apples
2lb (900g) tomatoes
12 oz (350g) soft brown sugar
3 large onions
1 pint (550ml) vinegar
1 tsp ground allspice
1 tsp salt
1 tsp ground cinnamon
1 tsp ground chillies
8 oz (225g) raisins
1 tsp ground cumin

Oven:

Simmering oven, 130C, 250F, Gas 1 and floor of roasting oven

Prepare in advance:

Pickle needs about a month to mature before eating

Freeze:

No need!

1 Wash six jam jars and put them, still wet, into the simmering oven.
2 Chop the tomatoes. Peel, core and grate the apples and onions. Remove the stalks from the chillies and peel the garlic: then whizz or finely chop them, together with the vinegar, spices and salt.
3 Put everything into a large preserving pan, bring to the boil then cover and move to the simmering oven for 3 hours.
4 When the vegetables are all soft, remove lid from the pan and put it onto the floor of the roasting oven to boil and reduce for a further hour, until thickened. Pour into the sterile jars and seal the tops.
5 Eat carefully, after about 4 weeks, or around Hallowe'en!

Tip: Seal the lids of the jars with cellophane discs or cling film between the top of the jar and the metal lid – otherwise the vinegar will corrode the metal jar lids

index